QUALI 2013
Abschluss-Prüfungsaufgaben mit Lösungen

Englisch
Bayern
2007–2012

STARK

Bildnachweis:
2008-6: © http://commons.wikimedia.org/wiki/Image:Harry_Potter_lines_Enhanced.jpg, lizensiert unter der GNU Free Documentation License Version 1.2 oder später

ISBN 978-3-8490-0073-8

© 2012 by Stark Verlagsgesellschaft mbH & Co. KG
23. ergänzte Auflage
www.stark-verlag.de

Das Werk und alle seine Bestandteile sind urheberrechtlich geschützt. Jede vollständige oder teilweise Vervielfältigung, Verbreitung und Veröffentlichung bedarf der ausdrücklichen Genehmigung des Verlages.

Inhalt

Vorwort

Hinweise und Tipps zum Quali

1 Ablauf der Prüfung I
2 Inhalte I
3 Leistungsanforderungen II
4 Methodische Hinweise und allgemeine Tipps zur Prüfung II
5 Bewertung III
6 Mündliche Prüfung IV

Kurzgrammatik

1 Adverbien – *adverbs* .... G 1
2 Bedingungssätze – *conditional sentences* .... G 2
3 Fürwörter – *pronouns* .... G 4
4 Grundform – *infinitive* .... G 5
5 Indirekte Rede – *reported speech* .... G 6
6 Modale Hilfsverben – *modal auxiliaries* .... G 8
7 Konjunktionen – *conjunctions* .... G 9
8 Partizipien – *participles* .... G 10
9 Passiv .... G 12
10 Relativsätze – *relative clauses* .... G 13
11 Steigerung und Vergleich – *comparisons* .... G 13
12 Wortstellung – *word order* .... G 15
13 Zeiten – *tenses* .... G 16
14 Liste wichtiger unregelmäßiger Verben – *list of irregular verbs* .... G 23

Übungsaufgaben

Listening Comprehension Test 1
Listening Comprehension Text: E-mail from Munich 2
Language Test 3
Reading Comprehension Test 16
Reading Comprehension Text: Action on wheels 16
Text Production 18
Letter 18
Picture Story 19
Mündliche Prüfung 20
Oral Report 20
Expressive Reading 20
Guided Dialogue 21

Schriftliche Abschlussprüfungsaufgaben

Übungsaufgabe im Stil des Quali Ü-1
Abschlussprüfung 2007 .... E 2007-1
Abschlussprüfung 2008 .... E 2008-1
Abschlussprüfung 2009 .... E 2009-1
Abschlussprüfung 2010 .... E 2010-1
Abschlussprüfung 2011 .... E 2011-1
Abschlussprüfung 2012 .... E 2012-1

Jeweils im Herbst erscheinen die neuen Ausgaben der Abschluss-Prüfungen an Hauptschulen

Hinweis: Die Übungsaufgaben zum Language Test, zum Reading Comprehension Test und zur Text Production wurden aus Abschlussprüfungsaufgaben der Jahrgänge vor 2001 zusammengestellt.

Autoren: Birgit Mohr, Redaktion (Kurzgrammatik)

Vorwort

Liebe Schülerin, lieber Schüler,

mit diesem Buch kannst du dich gezielt auf den Quali im Fach Englisch vorbereiten. Der Aufbau des Buches sieht so aus:

- In der **Kurzgrammatik** werden alle für die Prüfung wichtigen grammatischen Themen knapp erläutert und an Beispielsätzen veranschaulicht. Hier kannst du nachschlagen, wenn du einmal in der Grammatik unsicher sein solltest.

- Die **Übungsaufgaben zur schriftlichen Prüfung** erlauben es dir, gezielt auf einen Prüfungsteil hinzuarbeiten. Mit den **Übungsaufgaben zur mündlichen Prüfung** kannst du dich auch auf diesen Prüfungsteil optimal vorbereiten.

- Anhand der **schriftlichen Abschluss-Prüfungsaufgaben** der Jahre 2007 bis 2012 kannst du trainieren, die Prüfung im Ganzen zu bearbeiten, und dich so bestmöglich auf den schriftlichen Teil des Quali vorbereiten. Außerdem gibt es eine Übungsaufgabe im Stil des Quali.

Sollten nach Erscheinen dieses Bandes noch wichtige Änderungen in der Abschlussprüfung 2013 vom Kultusministerium bekannt gegeben werden, findest du aktuelle Informationen dazu im Internet unter:
www.stark-verlag.de/info.asp?zentrale-pruefung-aktuell

Viel Erfolg im Quali wünscht dir

Birgit Mohr

Hinweise und Tipps zum Quali

1 Ablauf der Prüfung

Am Ende der 9. Klasse kannst du in verschiedenen Fächern an einer besonderen Leistungsfeststellung teilnehmen, um zusätzlich zum „erfolgreichen Hauptschulabschluss" den „Qualifizierenden Hauptschulabschluss" zu erwerben. An dieser Leistungsfeststellung können auch externe Bewerber einer anderen Schulart teilnehmen. Die Leistungsfeststellung im Fach Englisch besteht sowohl aus einer **schriftlichen** als auch aus einer **mündlichen Prüfung**. Nur der schriftliche Teil der Prüfung ist zentral gestellt und ist somit für alle Schülerinnen und Schüler in Bayern gleich. Der mündliche Teil wird von Lehrkräften der Schule, an der du die Prüfung ablegst, ausgearbeitet und kann von Schule zu Schule verschieden sein. Besonders für externe Teilnehmer ist es wichtig, sich rechtzeitig an der zuständigen Haupt-/Mittelschule über die genauen Prüfungsanforderungen zu informieren.

Erlaubte Hilfsmittel
In der schriftlichen Prüfung darfst du für die Teile *Reading Comprehension* und *Text Production* ein zweisprachiges Wörterbuch verwenden. Über zugelassene Hilfsmittel in der mündlichen Prüfung entscheidet die Prüfungskommission der jeweiligen Schule. Erkundige dich rechtzeitig bei deinem Fachlehrer/deiner Fachlehrerin, wie die Bedingungen an deiner Schule genau aussehen.

2 Inhalte

Die Leistungsfeststellung im Fach Englisch setzt sich aus den folgenden Teilen und Kompetenzbereichen zusammen: Zunächst eine **schriftliche Prüfung, die aus den Kompetenzbereichen** *Listening Comprehension Test, Use of English, Reading Comprehension Test* und *Text Production* besteht. Für die Bearbeitung der beiden ersten Teile sind insgesamt **30 Minuten** vorgesehen. Es können **50 % der Gesamtpunktzahl** der schriftlichen Prüfung erreicht werden. Für die Bearbeitung der beiden letzten Teile stehen **60 Minuten** zur Verfügung. Auch in diesen Bereichen kann etwa die **Hälfte der Gesamtpunktzahl** erzielt werden. Außerdem gibt es eine mündliche Prüfung, die von den Schulen gestellt wird.

3 Leistungsanforderungen

Schriftliche Prüfung

Listening Comprehension Test: Ein Gespräch oder ein bzw. mehrere Texte werden von der CD abgespielt. Es folgen Aufgaben, die das Textverständnis überprüfen. Hier musst du als richtige Antwort das korrekte Ende eines Satzes ankreuzen *(multiple choice)* oder du musst entscheiden, ob eine Aussage über den gehörten Text richtig oder falsch ist *(true/false)*.

Use of English: In diesem Teil werden dein Wortschatz, deine Grammatikkenntnisse und deine Ausdrucksfähigkeit getestet. Diese Fähigkeiten werden z. B. mit Lückentexten überprüft, in die du das richtige Wort einsetzen musst oder es müssen die Teile eines Satzes in die richtige Reihenfolge gebracht werden. Außerdem können dir hier auch wieder *multiple choice*-Aufgaben begegnen.

Reading Comprehension Test: Hier erhältst du einen oder mehrere Texte zum Lesen. Anhand von Aufgaben wird das Leseverständnis überprüft. Hier musst du wieder die korrekte Antwort ankreuzen *(multiple choice)*. Zusätzlich können Fragen zum Text gestellt werden, die du in kurzen Sätzen beantworten sollst.

Text Production: Du kannst hier zwischen dem Schreiben einer *Correspondence* (E-Mail, Brief, Bewerbung) und dem *Picture Based Writing* (Bildergeschichte) wählen. Bei beiden Wahlmöglichkeiten werden dir Vorgaben gemacht, anhand derer du deinen Text verfasst.

Mündliche Prüfung

Die mündliche Prüfung dauert insgesamt **15 Minuten**. Sie kann von mehreren Schülern gleichzeitig absolviert werden. Sie enthält meist eine Auswahl der folgenden Prüfungsteile:
- *Opening Talk*: einleitendes Gespräch zwischen Schüler und Lehrer
- *Picture Based Communication*: Gespräch, dem ein Bild als Grundlage dient
- *Interpreting*: Übung zum Dolmetschen
- *Reacting to Prompts:* Gespräch, das durch inhaltliche Vorgaben gesteuert wird
- *Oral Report*: mündliches Referat mit anschließenden Fragen
- *Expressive Reading and Discourse*: Vorlesen eines englischen Textes, Fragen zum Textinhalt

4 Methodische Hinweise und allgemeine Tipps zur Prüfung

Vorbereitung
- Bereite dich **langfristig** vor. Das Buch enthält eine **Übersicht** über die verschiedenen **Kompetenzbereiche**, die in der Prüfung vorkommen. So kannst du dich gezielt mit Übungen aus diesem Buch auf die Prüfung vorbereiten.
- Übe **unter** möglichst „echten" **Prüfungsbedingungen:** Versuche, die Übungen in der dafür **vorgegebenen Zeit** zu schaffen. Wenn du die Übungen zunächst nicht in dieser Zeit lösen kannst, solltest du die Prüfungsaufgaben in regelmäßigen Ab-

ständen wiederholen, bis du sicherer und schneller wirst. Versuche stets, alle Aufgaben **selbstständig** zu lösen. Solltest du einmal gar nicht weiterkommen, kann ein Blick in die Lösung hilfreich sein, da dort wichtige **Hinweise und Tipps** zur Bearbeitung der Aufgabe gegeben werden. Vergleiche zum Schluss deine Lösung mit der Musterlösung und suche gegebenenfalls nach Rechtschreib- oder Grammatikfehlern.

In der Prüfung
Schriftliche Prüfung
- **Lies** die Aufgabenstellung **genau** durch.
- Überlege, auf welchen **Kompetenzbereich** (z. B. „Leseverstehen") sich die Aufgabe bezieht. Welche **Methoden** (z. B. Unterstreichen von wichtigen Textstellen) kennst du für diesen Bereich?
- Im Teilbereich *Use of English* findest du in der Prüfung zu den Aufgaben jeweils ein **Lösungsbeispiel** zur Verdeutlichung der Aufgabenstellung.

Mündliche Prüfung
- Befolge die Anweisungen der Prüfer und reagiere auf ihre **Anregungen**.
- Bereite den *Oral Report* **sorgfältig** vor.
- Versuche möglichst **umfangreiche** Antworten zu geben und das Gespräch „am Laufen" zu halten.

5 Bewertung

Die Bewertung deiner Leistung in der schriftlichen und mündlichen Prüfung erfolgt durch **zwei Lehrkräfte**. Die Noten, die du im schriftlichen und mündlichen Teil der Prüfung erzielst, werden 1:1 gewichtet, zählen also **gleichwertig**. Für die **schriftliche** Prüfung im Fach Englisch gilt eine einheitliche Zuordnung von erreichter Punktzahl und Note, die für alle bayerischen Schulen **verbindlich** ist. In der **mündlichen Prüfung** erfolgt die Notenvergabe nach **schulinternen** Maßstäben. Den Qualifizierenden Hauptschulabschluss hast du erlangt, wenn du in den Fächern der Leistungsfeststellung eine Gesamtbewertung von mindestens **3,0** erzielt hast.

Die Gesamtnotenpunkte setzen sich aus den Noten des Jahresfortgangs (diese Noten werden zu Beginn der Leistungsfeststellung ermittelt) und den Noten der Leistungsfeststellung zusammen. Die Fächer Deutsch, Mathematik sowie ein Fach aus Englisch/GSE/PCB zählen jeweils doppelt. Sämtliche Notenpunkte werden addiert und ergeben die Gesamtnotenpunktzahl. Je niedriger diese ist, desto besser ist die Endnote. Die Gesamtnotenpunktzahl wird durch 18 geteilt. Dabei ergibt sich die Endnote, deren zweite Stelle nach dem Komma nicht berücksichtigt wird. Den Qualifizierenden Hauptschulabschluss hast du geschafft, wenn du **maximal 55 Notenpunkte** bekommen hast ($55 : 18 = 3{,}05 \rightarrow 3{,}0$). Bei Externen und Schülern einer M-Klasse werden nur die Notenpunkte der Leistungsfeststellung gezählt. Der Teiler für die Gesamtpunktzahl ist dann 9.

6 Mündliche Prüfung

Zusätzlich zum festen Prüfungsteil „Mündliche Prüfung" gibt es noch eine weitere Möglichkeit der mündlichen Überprüfung deiner Kenntnisse: wenn du die oben genannten Voraussetzungen für den Erwerb des Qualifizierenden Hauptschulabschluss nicht erfüllt hast, kannst du dich zusätzlich einer mündlichen Prüfung in den Fächern **Deutsch und/oder Mathematik** unterziehen. Bei **56 oder 57 Notenpunkten** kannst du das Prüfungsergebnis noch verbessern und den Qualifizierenden Hauptschulabschluss erlangen, wenn du die zusätzliche mündliche Prüfung in den Fächern Deutsch **oder** Mathematik ablegst. Bei **58 oder 59 Notenpunkten** musst du die zusätzliche mündliche Prüfung in den Fächern Deutsch **und** Mathematik ablegen. Die Note der **Leistungsfeststellung** zählt **doppelt**, die Note der **zusätzlichen mündlichen Prüfung** zählt **einfach**.

Die Teilnahme an dieser zusätzlichen mündlichen Prüfung ist nur dann Erfolg versprechend, wenn das Ergebnis der mündlichen Prüfung **um mindestens 2 Notenstufen** über dem Ergebnis der schriftlichen Leistungsfeststellung liegt (z. B. Leistungsfeststellung Mathematik: Note 5; zusätzliche mündliche Prüfung Mathematik: Note 3). **Ansonsten ist keine Notenverbesserung zu erreichen.**

Kurzgrammatik

1 Adverbien – *adverbs*

Bildung Adjektiv + *-ly*	glad → glad<u>ly</u>
Ausnahmen:	
• *-y* am Wortende wird zu *-i*	eas<u>y</u> → eas<u>i</u>ly funn<u>y</u> → funn<u>i</u>ly
• auf einen Konsonanten folgendes *-le* wird zu *-ly*	simp<u>le</u> → simp<u>ly</u> terrib<u>le</u> → terrib<u>ly</u>
• am Wortende wird *-ic* zu *-ically*	fantas<u>tic</u> → fantas<u>tically</u>
Beachte:	
• In einigen Fällen haben Adjektiv und Adverb dieselbe Form.	daily, early, fast, hard, long, low, weekly, yearly
• Unregelmäßig gebildet wird:	good → well
• Endet das Adjektiv auf *-ly*, so kannst du kein Adverb bilden und verwendest deshalb: *in a* + Adjektiv + *manner*	friendly → <u>in a friendly</u> manner

Verwendung
Adverbien bestimmen z. B.

- Verben

  She <u>easily found</u> her way.
  Sie hat sich leicht zurechtgefunden.

- Adjektive oder

  This band is <u>extremely famous</u>.
  Diese Band ist sehr berühmt.

- andere Adverbien

  He walks <u>extremely quickly</u>.
  Er geht äußerst schnell.

näher.

Beachte: Nach bestimmten Verben (z. B. *to be, to become, to feel, to smell, to look*) steht ein Adjektiv.

Peter is funny.
Peter ist lustig.

I feel cold.
Mir ist kalt.

2 Bedingungssätze – *conditional sentences*

Ein Bedingungssatz besteht aus zwei Teilen: Nebensatz (*if*-Satz) + Hauptsatz. Im *if*-Satz steht die **Bedingung**, unter der die im **Hauptsatz** genannte **Folge** eintritt. Man unterscheidet drei Arten von Bedingungssätzen:

Bedingungssatz Typ I

Bildung
- *if*-Satz (Bedingung): Gegenwart *(simple present)*
- Hauptsatz (Folge): Zukunft mit *will (will-future)*

If you read this book,
Wenn du dieses Buch liest,
you will learn a lot about music.
erfährst du eine Menge über Musik.

Der *if*-Satz kann auch nach dem Hauptsatz stehen:
- Hauptsatz: *will-future*

- *if*-Satz: *simple present*

You will learn a lot about music
Du erfährst eine Menge über Musik,
if you read this book.
wenn du dieses Buch liest.

Im Hauptsatz kann statt dem *will-future* auch
- *can* + Grundform des Verbs,

If you go to London, you can see Bob.
Wenn du nach London fährst, kannst du Bob treffen.

- *must* + Grundform des Verbs,

If you go to London, you must visit me.
Wenn du nach London fährst, musst du mich besuchen.

- die Befehlsform (Imperativ)

stehen.

If it rains, take an umbrella.
Wenn es regnet, nimm einen Schirm mit.

Verwendung
Bedingungssätze vom Typ I verwendet man, wenn die **Bedingung erfüllbar** ist. Man gibt an, was unter bestimmten Bedingungen **geschieht, geschehen kann** oder was **geschehen sollte**.

Bedingungssatz Typ II

Bildung
- *if*-Satz (Bedingung):
  1. Vergangenheit *(simple past)*
- Hauptsatz (Folge): Konditional I
  (*conditional I = would +
  Grundform des Verbs*)

If I <u>went</u> to London,
Wenn ich nach London fahren würde,
I <u>would visit</u> the Tower of London.
würde ich mir den Tower of London ansehen.

Verwendung
Bedingungssätze vom Typ II verwendet man, wenn die **Bedingung theoretisch erfüllt** werden kann oder **nicht erfüllbar** ist.

Bedingungssatz Typ III

Bildung
- *if*-Satz (Bedingung):
  Vorvergangenheit *(past perfect)*
- Hauptsatz (Folge): Konditional II
  (*conditional II = would + have + past participle*)

If I <u>had gone</u> to London,
Wenn ich nach London gefahren wäre,
I <u>would have visited</u> the Tower of London.
hätte ich mir den Tower of London angesehen.

Verwendung
Bedingungssätze vom Typ III verwendet man, wenn sich die **Bedingung auf die Vergangenheit bezieht** und deshalb **nicht mehr erfüllbar** ist.

3 Fürwörter – *pronouns*

Besitzanzeigende Fürwörter – *possessive pronouns*

Besitzanzeigende Fürwörter *(possessive pronouns)* verwendet man, um zu sagen, **wem etwas gehört**. Steht ein besitzanzeigendes Fürwort allein, verwendest du eine andere Form:

mit Substantiv	ohne Substantiv		
my	*mine*	This is my bike. –	This is mine.
your	*yours*	This is your bike. –	This is yours.
his / her / its	*his / hers / …*	This is her bike. –	This is hers.
our	*ours*	This is our bike. –	This is ours.
your	*yours*	This is your bike. –	This is yours.
their	*theirs*	This is their bike. –	This is theirs.

Rückbezügliche Fürwörter – *reflexive pronouns*

Die rückbezüglichen Fürwörter *(reflexive pronouns)* **beziehen sich auf das Subjekt** des Satzes **zurück**. Es handelt sich also um dieselbe Person.

myself
  I will buy myself a new car.
  Ich werde mir ein neues Auto kaufen.

yourself
  You will buy yourself a new car.

himself / herself / itself
  He will buy himself a new car.

ourselves
  We will buy ourselves a new car.

yourselves
  You will buy yourselves a new car.

themselves
  They will buy themselves a new car.

each other/one another

each other/one another ist unveränderlich. Es bezieht sich auf **zwei oder mehr Personen** und wird mit „sich (gegenseitig), einander" übersetzt.

Beachte:
Einige Verben stehen ohne *each other*, obwohl auf Deutsch mit „sich" übersetzt wird.

They looked at <u>each other</u> and laughed.
Sie schauten sich (gegenseitig) an und lachten.
oder:
Sie schauten einander an und lachten.

to meet	*sich treffen*
to kiss	*sich küssen*
to fall in love	*sich verlieben*

4 Grundform – *infinitive*

Die Grundform mit *to* steht nach

- bestimmten Verben, z. B.:

to agree	zustimmen
to choose	wählen
to decide	entscheiden
to expect	erwarten
to hope	hoffen
to offer	anbieten
to plan	planen
to promise	versprechen
to seem	scheinen
to want	wollen

He <u>decided</u> <u>to wait</u>.
Er beschloss zu warten.

- bestimmten Substantiven, z. B.:

idea	Idee
plan	Plan
wish	Wunsch

It was her <u>wish</u> <u>to marry</u> in November.
Es war ihr Wunsch, im November zu heiraten.

- bestimmten Adjektiven, z. B.:

certain	sicher
difficult	schwer, schwierig
easy	leicht
hard	schwer, schwierig

It was <u>difficult</u> <u>to follow</u> her.
Es war schwer, ihr zu folgen.

- den Fragewörtern *what, where, which, who, when, why, how* in einer indirekten Frage.

We knew <u>where</u> <u>to find</u> her.
Wir wussten, wo wir sie finden würden.

5 Indirekte Rede – *reported speech*

Die indirekte Rede verwendet man, um **wiederzugeben, was ein anderer gesagt** oder **gefragt hat.**

Bildung
Um die indirekte Rede zu bilden, benötigt man ein **Einleitungsverb**. Häufig verwendete Einleitungsverben sind:

to say, to tell, to add, to agree, to think, to ask, to want to know, to answer

In der indirekten Rede verändern sich die Fürwörter (Pronomen), in bestimmten Fällen auch die **Zeiten** und die **Orts-** und **Zeitangaben**.

- **Veränderung der Fürwörter:**
  persönliche Fürwörter:
  besitzanzeigende Fürwörter:
  hinweisende Fürwörter:

direkte Rede	indirekte Rede
I, you, we, you	he, she, they
my, your, our, your	his, her, their
this, these	that, those

- **Zeiten**
  Keine Veränderung, wenn das **Einleitungsverb** in der **Gegenwart** *(simple present)* oder im *present perfect* steht:

direkte Rede	indirekte Rede
Bob <u>says</u>, "I <u>love</u> dancing."	Bob <u>says</u> (that) he <u>loves</u> dancing.
Bob sagt: „Ich tanze sehr gerne."	*Bob sagt, er tanze sehr gerne.*

Die Zeit der direkten Rede wird in der indirekten Rede **um eine Zeitstufe zurückversetzt**, wenn das **Einleitungsverb** im *simple past* steht:

Bob <u>said</u>, "I <u>love</u> dancing."	Bob <u>said</u> (that) he <u>loved</u> dancing.
Bob sagte: „Ich tanze sehr gerne."	*Bob sagte, er tanze sehr gerne.*

direkte Rede	indirekte Rede		
simple present	*simple past*	Joe: "I <u>like</u> it."	Joe said he <u>liked</u> it.
simple past	*past perfect*	Joe: "I <u>liked</u> it."	Joe said he <u>had liked</u> it.
present perfect	*past perfect*	Joe: "I'<u>ve liked</u> it."	Joe said he <u>had liked</u> it.
will-future	*conditional I*	Joe: "I <u>will like</u> it."	Joe said he <u>would</u> like it.

- Veränderung der Orts- und Zeitangaben:

now	→	then
today	→	that day
yesterday	→	the day before
the day before yesterday	→	two days before
tomorrow	→	the following day
next week	→	the following week
here	→	there

Bildung der indirekten Frage

Häufige Einleitungsverben für die indirekte Frage sind *to ask* oder *to want to know*.

- Enthält die direkte Frage ein **Fragewort**, **bleibt** dieses in der indirekten Frage **erhalten**. Die **Umschreibung** mit *do/does/did* **entfällt** in der indirekten Frage.

  Tom: "<u>When did</u> they arrive?"
  Tom asked <u>when</u> they had arrived.
  Tom: „Wann sind sie angekommen?"
  Tom fragte, wann sie angekommen seien.

- Enthält die direkte Frage **kein Fragewort**, wird die indirekte Frage mit ***whether*** oder ***if*** eingeleitet:

  Tom: "Are they staying at the hotel?"
  Tom asked <u>if/ whether</u> they were staying at the hotel.
  Tom: „Übernachten sie im Hotel?"
  Tom fragte, ob sie im Hotel übernachten.

Befehle/Aufforderungen in der indirekten Rede
Häufige Einleitungsverben sind *to tell, to order* (Befehl), *to ask* (Aufforderung).

In der indirekten Rede steht hier **Einleitungsverb + Objekt + (not) to + Grundform des Verbs** der direkten Rede.	Tom: "Leave the room." *Tom: „Verlass den Raum."*	Tom <u>told</u> <u>me</u> <u>to</u> <u>leave</u> the room. *Tom forderte mich auf, den Raum zu verlassen.*

6 Modale Hilfsverben – *modal auxiliaries*

Zu den **modalen Hilfsverben** *(modal auxiliaries)* zählen z. B. *can, may* und *must*.

Bildung
- Die modalen Hilfsverben haben für alle Personen **nur eine Form**.

  I, you, he/she/it, we, you, they } must

- Auf das modale Hilfsverb folgt die **Grundform** des Verbs **ohne *to***.

  You <u>must</u> <u>listen</u> to my new CD.
  Du musst dir meine neue CD anhören.

- **Frage und Verneinung** werden **nicht** mit *do/does/did* umschrieben.

  <u>Can</u> you help me, please?
  Kannst du mir bitte helfen?

Die modalen Hilfsverben können nicht alle Zeiten bilden. Deshalb benötigt man bestimmte **Ersatzformen**. Diese Ersatzformen können auch im Präsens verwendet werden.

- *can* (können)
  Ersatzformen:
  (to) be able to (Fähigkeit),
  (to) be allowed to (Erlaubnis)

  I <u>can</u> sing. / I <u>was able to</u> sing.
  Ich kann singen. / Ich konnte singen.
  You <u>can't</u> go to the party. /
  I <u>wasn't allowed to</u> go to the party.
  Du darfst nicht auf die Party gehen./
  Ich durfte nicht auf die Party gehen.

Im *simple past* und *conditional I* kannst du auch *could* verwenden.

- **may** (dürfen)
  Ersatzform: *(to) be allowed to*

I could sing.
Ich konnte singen.

You may go home early today. / You were allowed to go home early yesterday.
Du darfst heute früh nach Hause gehen. / Du durftest gestern früh nach Hause gehen.

- **must** (müssen)
  Ersatzform: *(to) have to*

  Beachte:
  must not/mustn't = „nicht dürfen"

  „nicht müssen, nicht brauchen" = **not have to, needn't**

He must be home by ten o'clock. / He had to be home by ten o'clock.
Er muss bis zehn Uhr zu Hause sein. / Er musste bis zehn Uhr zu Hause sein.

You must not eat all the cake.
Du darfst nicht den ganzen Kuchen essen.

You don't have to / needn't eat all the cake.
Du musst nicht den ganzen Kuchen essen. / Du brauchst nicht ... zu essen.

7 Konjunktionen – *conjunctions*

Konjunktionen *(conjunctions)* sind Bindewörter, die **zwei Hauptsätze oder Haupt- und Nebensatz miteinander verbinden**. Mit Konjunktionen lässt sich ein Text strukturieren, indem man z. B. Ursachen, Folgen oder zeitliche Abfolgen angibt. Hier findest du einige Beispiele für Konjunktionen:

after	– nachdem	What will you do after she's gone? *Was wirst du tun, nachdem sie gegangen ist?*
although	– obwohl	I like my bike although it's old. *Ich mag mein Fahrrad, obwohl es alt ist.*
because	– weil	I need a new bike because my old bike was stolen. *Ich brauche ein neues Rad, weil mein altes Rad gestohlen wurde.*

before	– bevor		Before he goes to work, he buys a newspaper. *Bevor er zur Arbeit geht, kauft er eine Zeitung.*
but	– aber		She likes football but she doesn't like skiing. *Sie mag Fußball, aber sie fährt nicht gerne Ski.*
that	– dass		It is nice that you are here. *Es ist schön, dass du hier bist.*
then	– dann		He bought an ice cream, and then shared it with Sally. *Er kaufte ein Eis, (und) dann teilte er es mit Sally.*
when	– wenn, als (zeitlich)		Tell me when you've finished. *Sag mir, wenn du fertig bist.* It rained when I was in Paris. *Es regnete, als ich in Paris war.*
while	– während, solange		While we were in London, we had very good weather. *Während wir in London waren, hatten wir sehr gutes Wetter.*

8 Partizipien – *participles*

Partizip Präsens – *present participle*

Bildung
Grundform des Verbs + *-ing*   read → read*ing*

Beachte:
- Stummes *-e* entfällt.   write → writ*ing*
- Verdoppelung des Schlusskonsonanten nach kurzem Vokal   stop → sto*pp*ing
- *-ie* wird zu *-y*.   l*ie* → l*y*ing

Verwendung
Das Partizip Präsens *(present participle)* verwendet man u. a.

- zur Bildung der Verlaufsform der Gegenwart *(present progressive)*,

  Peter <u>is reading</u>.
  Peter liest (gerade).

- zur Bildung der Verlaufsform der Vergangenheit *(past progressive)*.

  She <u>was reading</u> when I came back.
  Sie las (gerade), als ich zurückkam.

- wie ein Adjektiv, wenn es vor einem Substantiv steht.

  The village hasn't got <u>running</u> water.
  Das Dorf hat kein fließendes Wasser.

Partizip Perfekt – past *participle*

Bildung
Grundform des Verbs + *-ed*   talk → talk<u>ed</u>

Beachte:

- Stummes *-e* entfällt.   liv<u>e</u> → liv<u>ed</u>
- Nach kurzem betontem Vokal wird der Schlusskonsonant verdoppelt.   sto<u>p</u> → sto<u>pp</u>ed

- *-y* wird zu *-ie*.   cr<u>y</u> → cr<u>ie</u>d

- Unregelmäßige Verben: siehe Liste S. G 23 f. Hier sind bereits die *past-participle*-Formen der wichtigsten unregelmäßigen Verben angegeben:

  be → been
  have → had
  give → given
  go → gone

Verwendung
Das Partizip Perfekt *(past participle)* verwendet man u. a.

- zur Bildung des *present perfect*,

  He <u>hasn't talked</u> to his father yet.
  Er hat noch nicht mit seinem Vater gesprochen.

- zur Bildung des *past perfect*,

  Before they went to France, they <u>had bought</u> new bikes.
  Bevor sie nach Frankreich fuhren, hatten sie neue Fahrräder gekauft.

- zur Bildung des Passivs.

  The fish was <u>eaten</u> by the cat.
  Der Fisch wurde von der Katze gefressen.

- wie ein Adjektiv, wenn es vor einem Substantiv steht.

  Peter has got a well-<u>paid</u> job.
  Peter hat eine gut bezahlte Stelle.

9 Passiv

Bildung
Form von *(to) be* + Partizip Perfekt

The bridge <u>was finished</u> in 1894.
Die Brücke wurde 1894 fertiggestellt.

- im *simple present*

  Aktiv: Joe <u>buys</u> the milk.
  Passiv: The milk <u>is</u> <u>bought</u> by Joe.

- im *simple past*

  Aktiv: Joe <u>bought</u> the milk.
  Passiv: The milk <u>was</u> <u>bought</u> by Joe.

Aktiv → Passiv

Bei der Umwandlung vom Aktiv ins Passiv ...

- ... wird das Subjekt des Aktivsatzes zum Objekt des Passivsatzes. Es wird mit *by* angeschlossen *(by-agent)*.

- ... wird das Objekt des Aktivsatzes zum Subjekt des Passivsatzes.

Aktiv: Joe   buys   the milk.
          Subjekt   *Objekt*

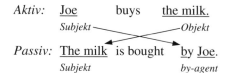

Passiv: The milk   is bought   by Joe.
          Subjekt   *by-agent*

10 Relativsätze – *relative clauses*

Ein Relativsatz ist ein Nebensatz, der sich auf eine **Person oder Sache des Hauptsatzes** bezieht und diese **näher beschreibt**:
- Hauptsatz:
- Relativsatz:

The boy who looks like Jane is her brother.
Der Junge, der Jane ähnlich sieht, ist ihr Bruder.

The boy ... is her brother
... who looks like Jane ...

Bildung
Haupt- und Nebensatz werden durch ein Relativpronomen *(who, which, that)* verbunden.

- *who* bezieht sich auf **Personen**,

Peter, who lives in London, likes travelling.
Peter, der in London lebt, reist gerne.

- *which* bezieht sich auf **Sachen**,

The film "Dark Moon", which we saw yesterday, was far too long.
Der Film „Dark Moon", den wir gestern sahen, war viel zu lang.

- *that* kann sich auf **Sachen** und in der Umgangssprache auch auf **Personen** beziehen.

The film that we saw last week was much better.
Der Film, den wir letzte Woche sahen, war viel besser.

11 Steigerung und Vergleich – *comparisons*

Steigerung des Adjektivs – *comparison of adjectives*

Bildung
Man unterscheidet:
- Grundform
- 1. Steigerungsform (Komparativ)
- 2. Steigerungsform (Superlativ)

Peter is young.
Jane is younger.
Paul is the youngest.

Steigerung auf -er, -est
Bei den meisten einsilbigen und zweisilbigen Adjektiven, z. B.:

old, old<u>er</u>, old<u>est</u>
alt, älter, am ältesten

funny, funn<u>ier</u>, funn<u>iest</u>
lustig, lustiger, am lustigsten

Beachte:
- stummes *-e* am Wortende entfällt
- nach einem Konsonanten wird *-y* am Wortende zu *-i-*
- nach kurzem Vokal wird ein Konsonant am Wortende verdoppelt

simpl<u>e</u>, simpl<u>er</u>, simpl<u>est</u>

funn<u>y</u>, funn<u>ier</u>, funn<u>iest</u>

fi<u>t</u>, fi<u>tt</u>er, fi<u>tt</u>est

Steigerung mit *more ..., most ...*
- zweisilbige Adjektive, die nicht auf *-er, -le, -ow* oder *-y* enden
- Adjektive mit drei und mehr Silben

useful, <u>more</u> useful, <u>most</u> useful
nützlich, nützlicher, am nützlichsten

difficult, <u>more</u> difficult, <u>most</u> difficult
schwierig, schwieriger, am schwierigsten

Unregelmäßige Steigerung
Die unregelmäßig gesteigerten Adjektive solltest du lernen. Einige wichtige Adjektive sind hier angegeben.

good, better, best
gut, besser, am besten

bad, worse, worst
schlecht, schlechter, am schlechtesten

many, more, most
viele, mehr, am meisten

much, more, most
viel, mehr, am meisten

little, less, least
wenig, weniger, am wenigsten

Vergleiche von Personen und Dingen

Bildung

- Wenn du sagen möchtest, dass Personen oder Dinge **gleich** sind:
  as + Adjektiv (Grundform) + *as*

  Anne is <u>as</u> <u>tall</u> <u>as</u> John.
  Anne ist genauso groß wie John.

- Wenn du sagen möchtest, dass Personen oder Dinge **ungleich** sind: *not as* + Adjektiv (Grundform) + *as*

  John is <u>not as</u> <u>tall</u> <u>as</u> Steve.
  John ist nicht so groß wie Steve.

- Wenn du sagen möchtest, dass Personen oder Dinge **verschieden** gut/schlecht/schön ... sind:
  1. Steigerungsform (Komparativ) des Adjektivs + *than*

  Steve is <u>taller</u> <u>than</u> Anne.
  Steve ist größer als Anne.

Steigerung des Adverbs – *comparison of adverbs*

Adverbien können wie Adjektive ebenfalls gesteigert werden.

- Adverbien auf *-ly* werden mit **more, most** bzw. mit **less, least** gesteigert.

  She talks <u>more</u> <u>quickly</u> than John.
  Sie spricht schneller als John.

- Adverbien, die dieselbe Form wie das Adjektiv haben, werden mit *-er, -est* gesteigert.

  fast – fast<u>er</u> – fast<u>est</u>
  early – earl<u>ier</u> – earl<u>iest</u>

- Folgende Adverbien haben unregelmäßige Steigerungsformen:

  well – better – best
  badly – worse – worst

12 Wortstellung – *word order*

Im englischen Aussagesatz gilt die Wortstellung <u>Subjekt</u> – <u>Prädikat</u> – <u>Objekt</u> *(subject – verb – object)*:

- Das Subjekt gibt an, wer oder was etwas tut.

  The cat
  Die Katze

- Das Prädikat gibt an, was getan wird.

  catches
  fängt

- Das Objekt gibt an, worauf/auf wen sich die Tätigkeit bezieht.

  a mouse.
  eine Maus.

Beachte:
- Orts- und Zeitangaben stehen meist am Satzende.

  We will buy a new car tomorrow.
  Morgen kaufen wir ein neues Auto.
  Peter lives in New York.
  Peter wohnt in New York.

- Ortsangaben stehen vor Zeitangaben.

  He moved to Paris in June.
  Er ist im Juni nach Paris gezogen.

13 Zeiten – *tenses*

Gegenwart – *simple present*

Bildung
Grundform des Verbs,
Ausnahme 3. Person Singular:
Grundform des Verbs + -s

stand   –   he/she/it stands

Beachte:
- Bei Verben, die auf -s, -sh, -ch, -x enden, wird -es angefügt.

  kiss   –   he/she/it kisses
  rush   –   he/she/it rushes
  teach   –   he/she/it teaches
  fix   –   he/she/it fixes

- Bei Verben, die auf Konsonant + -y enden, wird -es angefügt; -y wird zu -i-.

  carry   –   he/she/it carries

Bildung von Fragen im *simple present*
(Fragewort +) *do/does* + Grundform des Verbs

Where does he live? / Does he live in London?
Wo lebt er? / Lebt er in London?

Beachte:
Die Umschreibung mit *do/does* wird nicht verwendet,
- wenn nach dem Subjekt gefragt wird (mit *who, what, which*).

Who came to the party?
Wer kam zur Party?
What happens next?
Was passiert als Nächstes?

- wenn die Frage mit *is/are* gebildet wird.

Are you happy?
Bist du glücklich?

Bildung der Verneinung im *simple present*
don't/doesn't + Grundform des Verbs

He doesn't like football.
Er mag Fußball nicht.

Verwendung
Das *simple present* beschreibt
- Tätigkeiten, die man **gewohnheitsmäßig** oder häufig (oder gar nicht) ausführt.
  Signalwörter: z. B. *always, often, never, every day, every morning*

Every morning John buys a newspaper.
Jeden Morgen kauft sich John eine Zeitung.

- **allgemeingültige** Aussagen.

London is a big city.
London ist eine große Stadt.

- **Eigenschaften** und **Zustände** von Personen und Dingen, z. B. *to like, to hate, to know*

I like dogs.
Ich mag Hunde.

- ein **zukünftiges Geschehen** mit einem festen Termin (z. B. Fahrpläne, Kalender).

The train leaves at 8.15.
Der Zug fährt um 8.15 Uhr.
The holidays start next week.
Nächste Woche fangen die Ferien an.

Verlaufsform des *simple present* – *present progressive/continuous*

Bildung
am/is/are + Verb in der *-ing*-Form (Partizip Präsens)

read → am/is/are reading

Bildung von Fragen im *present progressive* (Fragewort +) *am/is/are* + Subjekt + Verb in der *-ing*-Form	Is Peter reading? / What is he reading? *Liest Peter gerade? / Was liest er?*
Bildung der Verneinung im *present progressive* *am not/isn't/aren't* + Verb in der *-ing*-Form	Peter isn't reading. *Peter liest gerade nicht.*

Verwendung Mit dem *present progressive* drückt man aus,	
• dass etwas **gerade passiert** und **noch nicht abgeschlossen** ist. Signalwörter: *at the moment, now*	At the moment, Peter is drinking a cup of tea. *Im Augenblick trinkt Peter eine Tasse Tee. [Er hat damit angefangen und noch nicht aufgehört.]*
• dass es um eine **zukünftige Handlung** geht, die bereits **fest geplant** ist.	We are watching the match on Sunday. *Am Sonntag sehen wir uns das Spiel an.*

Simple past

Bildung Regelmäßige Verben: Grundform des Verbs + *-ed*	walk → walk<u>ed</u>
Beachte: • Stummes *-e* entfällt. • Bei Verben, die auf Konsonant + *-y* enden, wird *-y* zu *-i-*.	hop<u>e</u> → hop<u>ed</u> car<u>ry</u> → carr<u>ied</u>
• Nach kurzem betontem Vokal wird der Schlusskonsonant verdoppelt.	st<u>o</u>p → sto<u>pp</u>ed

Unregelmäßige Verben: siehe Liste S. G 23 f. Hier sind bereits die *simple past*-Formen der wichtigsten unregelmäßigen Verben angegeben:

be → was
have → had
give → gave
go → went

Bildung von Fragen im *simple past*
(Fragewort +) *did* + Grundform des Verbs

Did he look out of the window?
Why did he look out of the window?
Sah er aus dem Fenster?
Warum sah er aus dem Fenster?

Beachte:
Die Umschreibung mit *did* wird nicht verwendet,
- wenn nach dem Subjekt gefragt wird (mit *who, what, which*),

Who paid the bill?
Wer zahlte die Rechnung?

What happened to your friend?
Was ist mit deinem Freund passiert?

Which boy cooked the meal?
Welcher Junge kochte das Essen?

- wenn die Frage mit *was/were* gebildet wird.

Were you happy?
Warst du glücklich?

Bildung der Verneinung im *simple past*
didn't + Grundform des Verbs

He didn't call me.
Er hat mich nicht angerufen.

Verwendung
Das *simple past* beschreibt Handlungen und Ereignisse, die **in der Vergangenheit geschehen** und **bereits abgeschlossen** sind.

Last week he helped me with my homework.
Letzte Woche half er mir bei meinen Hausaufgaben. [Die Handlung (helfen) fand in der letzten Woche statt, ist also bereits abgeschlossen.]

Signalwörter: z. B. *yesterday, last week, (five years) ago, in 2008*

Verlaufsform des *simple past* – *past progressive/continuous*

Bildung
was/were + Verb in der -*ing*-Form

watch → was/were watching

Verwendung
Das *past progressive* verwendet man, wenn **zu einem bestimmten Zeitpunkt** in der Vergangenheit eine **Handlung ablief**, bzw. wenn eine **Handlung** von einer anderen **unterbrochen** wurde.

Yesterday at 11 o'clock I was still sleeping.
Gestern um 11 Uhr habe ich noch geschlafen.

I was reading a book when Peter came into the room.
Ich las (gerade) ein Buch, als Peter ins Zimmer kam.

Present perfect

Bildung
have/has + Partizip Perfekt

write → has/have written

Verwendung
Das *present perfect* verwendet man, wenn
- ein Vorgang **in der Vergangenheit begonnen** hat und **noch andauert**.

- das Ergebnis einer vergangenen Handlung **Auswirkungen auf die Gegenwart** hat.

Signalwörter: z. B. *already, ever, just, how long, not ... yet, since, for*

He has lived in London since 2008.
Er lebt seit 2008 in London.
[Er lebt jetzt immer noch in London.]

I have tidied up my room.
Ich habe mein Zimmer aufgeräumt.
[Jetzt sieht es wieder ordentlich aus.]

Beachte:
- *have/has* können zu *'ve/'s* verkürzt werden.

I've eaten your lunch.
Ich habe dein Mittagessen gegessen.

He's given me his umbrella.
Er hat mir seinen Schirm gegeben.

- Das *present perfect* wird oft mit *since* und *for* verwendet (Deutsch: „seit"):
  since gibt einen **Zeitpunkt** an:

  Ron has lived in Sydney since 1997.
  Ron lebt seit 1997 in Sydney.

- *for* gibt einen **Zeitraum** an:

  Sally has lived in Berlin for five years.
  Sally lebt seit fünf Jahren in Berlin.

Verlaufsform des *present perfect* – *present perfect progressive/continuous*

Bildung
have/has + been + Partizip Präsens

write → has/have been writing

Verwendung
Das *present perfect progressive* verwendet man, um die **Dauer einer Handlung** zu **betonen**, die in der Vergangenheit begonnen hat und noch andauert.

She has been sleeping for ten hours.
Sie schläft seit zehn Stunden.

Past perfect

Bildung
had + Partizip Perfekt

write → had written

Verwendung
Das *past perfect* verwendet man, wenn ein Vorgang in der Vergangenheit **vor einem anderen Vorgang in der Vergangenheit abgeschlossen** wurde.

He had bought a ticket
Er hatte ein Ticket gekauft,

before he took the train to Manchester.
bevor er den Zug nach Manchester nahm. [Beim Einsteigen war der Kauf abgeschlossen.]

Verlaufsform des *past perfect* – past perfect progressive/continuous

Bildung
had + *been* + Partizip Präsens

write → had been writing

Verwendung
Das *past perfect progressive* verwendet man für **Handlungen**, die in der Vergangenheit **bis zu dem Zeitpunkt andauerten**, zu dem eine neue Handlung einsetzte.

She had been sleeping for ten hours when the doorbell rang.
Sie hatte seit zehn Stunden geschlafen, als es an der Tür klingelte. [Sie schlief bis zu dem Zeitpunkt, als es an der Tür klingelte.]

Zukunft mit *will* – will-future

Bildung
will + Grundform des Verbs

buy → will buy

Bildung von Fragen im *will-future*
(Fragewort) + *will* + Grundform des Verbs

What will you buy?
Was wirst du kaufen?

Bildung der Verneinung im *will-future*
won't + Grundform des Verbs

Why won't you come to the party?
Warum kommst du nicht zur Party?

Verwendung
Das *will-future* verwendet man, wenn ein Vorgang **in der Zukunft stattfinden** wird:
- bei Vorhersagen oder Vermutungen,

The weather will be fine tomorrow.
Das wird morgen schön.

I think she will take the red dress.
Ich denke, sie nimmt das rote Kleid.

- bei spontanen Entscheidungen.

Ok, I'll do that.
Ok, ich werde es machen.

Signalwörter: z. B. *tomorrow, next week, next Monday, next year, in three years, soon*

Zukunft mit *going to* – *going-to-future*

Bildung
am/is/are + *going to* + Grundform des Verbs

find → am/is/are going to find

Verwendung
Das *going-to-future* verwendet man u. a., wenn man ausdrücken will, was man für die Zukunft **plant** oder **zu tun beabsichtigt**.

I am going to work in England this summer.
Diesen Sommer werde ich in England arbeiten.

14 Liste wichtiger unregelmäßiger Verben – *list of irregular verbs*

Infinitiv	Präteritum	Partizip	Deutsch
be	was / were	been	*sein*
become	became	become	*werden*
begin	began	begun	*beginnen*
break	broke	broken	*brechen*
bring	brought	brought	*bringen*
buy	bought	bought	*kaufen*
catch	caught	caught	*fangen*
come	came	come	*kommen*
do	did	done	*tun*
drink	drank	drunk	*trinken*
drive	drove	driven	*fahren*
eat	ate	eaten	*essen*
fall	fell	fallen	*fallen*
feel	felt	felt	*fühlen*
find	found	found	*finden*
forget	forgot	forgotten	*vergessen*
get	got	got	*bekommen*

Infinitiv	Präteritum	Partizip	Deutsch
give	gave	given	*geben*
go	went	gone	*gehen*
have	had	had	*haben*
hear	heard	heard	*hören*
hit	hit	hit	*schlagen*
hold	held	held	*halten*
know	knew	known	*wissen*
leave	left	left	*verlassen*
let	let	let	*lassen*
make	made	made	*machen*
meet	met	met	*treffen*
pay	paid	paid	*bezahlen*
put	put	put	*stellen/setzen*
read	read	read	*lesen*
run	ran	run	*rennen*
say	said	said	*sagen*
see	saw	seen	*sehen*
sell	sold	sold	*verkaufen*
send	sent	sent	*schicken*
show	showed	shown	*zeigen*
sit	sat	sat	*sitzen*
sleep	slept	slept	*schlafen*
speak	spoke	spoken	*sprechen*
spend	spent	spent	*ausgeben/ verbringen*
stand	stood	stood	*stehen*
take	took	taken	*nehmen*
tell	told	told	*erzählen*
think	thought	thought	*denken*
win	won	won	*gewinnen*
write	wrote	written	*schreiben*

Übungsaufgaben

Listening Comprehension Text

E-mail from Munich

Jamie liest Mark die E-Mail von Nicole, einer guten Freundin, vor:

Dear Jamie,

Here's your first mail from your friend Nicole! I have been in Munich for a week now and it is great fun. But I already miss England a lot: English weather, English football and most of all you and my other English friends!

Being an exchange student is very interesting. I have had a full week of school now and I have made some friends by now. I'm staying with Katja and her family. Katja does not speak English very well, but she is very nice to me. Her parents are nice and friendly, too. It's a pity that Katja has become ill now and can't go to school for a while.

So I am really happy that I have met Julia in my class. Julia is Katja's best friend. I sit next to Julia now and she helps me a lot, because my German is not so good yet. It's wonderful that everybody here speaks English so well! Julia's English is the best, because she lived in the US when she was younger, but she is German. I try to follow lessons as much as I can, but it is hard. It is not so difficult in maths, but it's hard in German and in history. Sometimes when I'm lost again, Julia helps me. We have a lot of fun in sports, because then we can play together and we talk a lot!

I try to speak as much German as I can. It is not so easy to talk German with real Germans, because they talk too fast and there are so many words that I don't know. But Katja and Julia speak slowly and use easy words.

Julia is giving a birthday party next Friday and has invited us. I don't know if Katja will be able to go, because she is ill, but Katja's parents have already told me that they will take me to the party and pick me up[4] again, even if Katja can't go.

Last weekend, when Katja was still feeling well, her parents took us on a tour of Munich. We looked at some historic buildings like the Frauenkirche, a big church with two towers, and the Opera house. We saw the English garden, but there was nothing very English about it. We had lunch at a big Bavarian restaurant. Then in the afternoon, we saw the Olympic Centre where they held the Olympic Games in 1972. Katja's parents told me that there is still a lot going on there, like soccer matches or rock concerts, but it was all quiet when we visited it.

But what I liked best was the city centre, where there are a lot of shops and department stores and where we did some shopping at the end of the tour.

Katja's parents have told me that we are going on a trip to the country next weekend and then I will see Neuschwanstein castle!

There is so much to see here and it would be great if you could be here, too. Please write back and tell me what is going on in England! Say hello to all the others for me!

Yours,
Nicole

1. **Underline the right word.**

   a) Nicole misses the English TV programmes/<u>weather</u>/food.

   b) Being an exchange student is <u>interesting</u>/intelligent/difficult.

   c) Nicole/<u>Katja</u>/Katja's father is ill.

   d) Julia lived in the UK/United Emirates/<u>US</u> when she was younger.

   e) It's hard to follow the lessons in sports/maths/<u>history</u>.

   f) Julia is having a picnic/<u>party</u>/tour next Friday.

   g) During their trip to Munich, Nicole visited <u>a church</u>/a soccer match/a rock concert.

   h) At the end of the tour they <u>went shopping</u>/to Neuschwanstein/to the country.

2. **One ending is correct for each of the following sentences. Tick it (✓).**

   a) Nicole has been in Munich
   - [ ] for a month.
   - [✓] for a week.
   - [ ] four weeks.

   b) Katja
   - [✓] isn't good at English.
   - [ ] isn't good at school.
   - [ ] isn't German.

   c) The best English is spoken by
   - [✓] Julia.
   - [ ] Katja.
   - [ ] the sports teacher.

   d) Nicole tries to speak
   - [ ] dialect.
   - [✓] a little German.
   - [ ] a lot of German.

   e) The Olympic Games were held in Munich in
   - [ ] 1970.
   - [✓] 1972.
   - [ ] 1927.

Abschlussprüfungen an Hauptschulen in Bayern – Englisch
Übungsaufgaben: Language Test

1. **Look at the label. Cross out the word that doesn't fit.**

    Example: made of fruit: jam – juice – ~~coat~~ – marmalade

    a) made of wood: pencil – ~~telephone~~ – cupboard – table
    b) made of cotton: gloves – shirt – stove – stockings
    c) made of glass: windscreen – bottle – ~~blanket~~ – mirror
    d) made of leather: handbag – purse – shoe – ~~socks~~

2. **Cross out the word that doesn't fit.**

    Example: jobs: dentist – chemist – florist – ~~tourist~~

    a) clothes: suit – tie – skirt – ~~skin~~
    b) meals: breakfast – dinner – ~~plate~~ – lunch
    c) parts of the body: shoulder – neck – ~~boot~~ – knee
    d) plants: ~~flour~~ – bush – grass – tree

3. **Find one more example and the collective noun.**

    Example: red – green – white – __blue__ : __colours__

    a) silver – copper – zinc – __gold__ : __metals__
    b) saw – drill – screwdriver – __hammer__ : __tools__
    c) fog – rain – sun – __snow__ : __weather__

4. **Give two examples for each collective noun.**

    a) vegetables: __tomato, potato__
    b) desserts: __cake, apple-pie__
    c) meat: __chicken, lamb__

5. **Cross out the word that doesn't fit and find the collective noun.**

    Example: cupboard – armchair – ~~book~~ – table – bed – desk → __furniture__

    a) cabbage – ~~pears~~ – beans – potatoes – carrots – peas → __vegetables__
    b) gloves – scarf – trousers – coat – skirt – ~~watch~~ → __clothes__
    c) neck – head – ~~food~~ – elbow – knee – ankle → __parts of the body__

6. What do you need to …

Example: … clean the living-room floor → vacuum cleaner

a) … cut bread → knife
b) … wash your jeans → washing machine
c) … lock the door → key
d) … clean your teeth → toothbrush

7. Where can you find these persons and things?

Example: menu – waiter – drinks: restaurant

a) planes – runways – gates: airport
b) receptionist – keys – rooms: hotel
c) mechanic – cars – tools: garage
d) sand – shells – waves: beach

8. Where do people usually do that?

Example: pray – church

a) study – college, university
b) change money – bank
c) catch a plane – airport
d) build cars – car factory
e) report a stolen car – police station
f) keep food cool – fridge

9. Name one thing in each sentence.

What do you learn in these school subjects?
Example: In mathematics we learn about numbers.

a) In geography we learn about countries.
b) In history we learn about famous people, king.
c) In biology we learn about nature, animals.
d) In social studies we learn about government, our city.

Übungsaufgaben: Language Test

10. In what countries are these languages spoken?

Example: Italian is spoken in _Italy_.
a) French is spoken in _France_.
b) Dutch is spoken in _Holland_.
c) Greek is spoken in _Greece_.
d) Norwegian is spoken in _Norway_.

11. Find another word with the same meaning.

Example: My brother is a hard-working student / _pupil_.
a) His English test was very hard / _difficult_.
b) He would be glad / _happy_ to get a good mark on it.
c) School will end / _finish_ at the end of July.
d) He hopes to get a gift / _present_ for a good school report.

12. Find the opposites.

Example: The Watsons' new flat is better than their _old_ one.
a) When he goes sailing, Hank enjoys the terrific air. The pollution in the town where he lives is _terrible_.
b) Noise and traffic make people ill, but Pam hopes that sport will keep her _healthy_.
c) Jill and John have the same kind of job, but they work at _different_ factories.
d) Phil has got a well-paid job, but he spends all the money he _earns, makes_.

13. Find the opposites of the underlined words.

Example: The film wasn't interesting. It was _boring_.
a) Learning to play the piano isn't easy, it's _difficult_.
b) Early in the morning Susan ran to the bus stop. But she didn't _catch_ the bus. She missed it.
c) Susan is very clever. She doesn't _spend_ all her money. She tries to save some.
d) Don't laugh like that. – Why not? Do you want me to _cry_?

14. Write down the feminine form.

Example: father – *mother*

a) son   – daughter
b) king   – queen
c) husband – wife
d) waiter – waitress

15. Put the following words into the plural form.

a) mouse – mice
b) child – children
c) lady – ladies
d) knife – knives

16. Find the adjectives.

Example: difference – *different*

a) health   – healthy
b) beauty   – beautiful
c) danger   – dangerous
d) activity – active

17. Fill in the right preposition. What has the police dog got to do?

a) The police dog has to climb __over__ the wall.
b) It has to crawl __under__ the barrier and
c) __through__ the tunnel.
d) Finally it has to jump into the water and swim __across__ the river.

18. Fill in the right preposition.

Example: The family is sitting ___at___ the table.

a) What's the difference ___between___ a lake and a pond?
b) Have you ever been ___in___ New York?
c) Where does the new pupil come ___from___?
d) What do you think ___about___ UFOs?

19. Choose the right word for the questions.

> what – when – why – where – how many – ~~who~~ – ~~which~~ – how much

A new girl in class

a) ___Who___ is that good-looking man over there? – He's Mr. Jones.
b) ___What___ does he teach? – English.
c) ___When___ is our first English lesson? – Today at 10 o'clock.
d) ___How many___ English lessons a week do we have? – Six.
e) ___Which___ of those cars is his? – I don't know.
f) ___How much___ money does he earn? – I don't know.
But you can go and ask him yourself.

20. Fill in the missing words.

Example: fish – swim, bird – fly

a) shirt – wear, suitcase – ___carry___
b) car – drive, bike – ___ride___
c) lemon – sour, sugar – ___sweet___
d) factory – worker, shop – ___(shop) assistant___

21. Choose the right verbs.

> become – carry – drive – get – ~~hear~~ – listen – look – ride – say – tell – ~~watch~~ – ~~wear~~

Sally is thinking about her birthday party next week:

"I'm going to ___wear___ my blue dress. I'm sure my friends would like to ___listen___ to the latest Hip Hop CD. Perhaps we'll ___watch___ a video on TV, too. I'm going to ___tell___ my friends some jokes as well. After the party my friends will ___ride___ home on their bikes. I wonder what presents I will ___get___."

Übungsaufgaben: Language Test

22. Fill in the right verb.

> wrote – caught – ate – was – were – broke – bought

a) Last week I __broke__ my leg.
b) It __was__ very boring in bed.
c) So my mother __bought__ me some comics.
d) And I __wrote__ some letters to my friends.

23. Put the verbs in brackets into the simple past.

On Monday morning Sally is telling her friend Sue about her weekend:

On Saturday evening I (go) __went__ to the cinema. On Sunday my boyfriend (invite) __invited__ me to dinner at a Chinese restaurant. I (put on) __put on__ my new dress. We (eat) __ate__ and (drink) __drank__ a lot. Later we (take) __took__ a taxi home. I (feel) __felt__ great when he kissed me on the doorstep.

24. Fill in the infinitive forms of the verbs.

Peter spent his holidays on his grandparents' farm. There he <u>repaired</u> the fence, he <u>rode</u> a horse, he <u>drove</u> a tractor, he <u>caught</u> some fish, he <u>fed</u> the chickens, he <u>threw</u> horseshoes (Hufeisen) and he <u>built</u> a doghouse.

Home again, he tells his parents:
"Now I can __repair__ a fence, I can __ride__ a horse and I can __drive__ a tractor. I learned how to __catch__ fish and how to __feed__ the chickens. Grandpa showed me how to __throw__ horseshoes and how to __build__ a doghouse."

25. Find the correct ending to each sentence.

a) At the moment…   1) … he jogs in Central Park.
b) Two years ago…   2) … Mr Jones is visiting a conference in New York.
c) Tomorrow…   3) … he slept in his car because he couldn't get a room in a hotel.
d) Every morning…   4) … he will watch a musical on Broadway.

26. Fill in the correct forms of the verbs.

Peter and George are talking about their holiday plans.

PETER: Oh, I've got a problem. I don't know where to go on holiday this year.
(fly) Last year I _flew_ to Italy with my parents.
(visit) Next year I'll _visit_ my cousin in Scotland. But this year?
GEORGE: Well, perhaps I can help you with your problem.
(be) _Have_ you ever _been_ to Austria?
I spent a cheap and really fantastic holiday there last summer.
PETER: (sound) Oh, that _sounds_ great!

27. Fill in the correct forms of the verbs.

a) (be) Jim _was_ in a motorbike accident two months ago.
b) (take) So he _takes_ the bus to work every day.
c) (buy) His father'll _buy_ him another bike for his next birthday.
d) (see) They _have_ already _seen_ a nice second-hand motorbike.

28. Mark the right meaning with a cross.

a) Sally always listens to the radio while doing her homework.
- [ ] She listens to the radio before she does her homework.
- [ ] She listens to the radio after she has done her homework.
- [x] She listens to the radio and does her homework at the same time.

b) If Sally has enough money, she will buy a stereo.
- [ ] Sally has bought a stereo.
- [x] Sally wants to buy a stereo.
- [x] Sally is going to buy a stereo.

c) Sally went to the radio shop after she had finished her homework.
- [x] Sally did her homework first.
- [ ] Sally went to the radio shop first.
- [ ] Sally had gone to the radio shop before she did her homework.

Übungsaufgaben: Language Test

29. Make negative sentences.

Barbara and Ann are talking about their boyfriends.
Barbara says: "Peter is a techno fan. He likes techno music a lot. Last weekend we bought tickets for a techno party. Next month we'll go to the techno hall." Ann says: "Bobby isn't a techno fan.

a) He doesn't like this kind of music.

b) Last weekend we didn't buy tickets for the techno party, but Bobby bought tickets for a rock concert.

c) I don't like rock at all, so I'm not going to the concert with him next week. He can go with his little brother."

30. Ask questions.

After Peter came back from his holiday in Austria, George asked him about it.

George: Peter:
a) Where did you stay?   At a camp-site, near a lake.
b) What was the weather like?   Sunny and warm.
c) How much it cost?   About £ 500.

31. Ask the question.

After a Western parade you meet another tourist.

Where are you from? – From L. A.
Frage ihn, wo er herkommt.

How long have you been here? – Since yesterday.
Frage ihn, wie lange er schon hier ist.

Did you like the show? – Yes, it was great.
Frage ihn, ob ihm die Vorstellung gefallen hat.

What _____ – I think I'll have dinner.
Frage ihn, was er als Nächstes vorhat.

32. Find the right form.

After their party, Susan and her friends are comparing it with some other parties.

a) (nice)   "Our party was much nicer than Mandy's party last week."

b) (loud)   "This year our neighbours did not complain, because the music was not as loud as last year."

c) (beautiful) "The decorations were the most beautiful we've ever had."

33. Finish these sentences.

The Dawsons are making plans for the weekend.
a) If it's warm next Sunday, we 'll go swimming.
b) If it rains, we 'll stay at home.

34. Fill in the right pronouns.

Example: The house is old – **Its** windows are broken.

The Millers moved to a new house because their flat had become too small. Mary and her sister Jane got a big room on the first floor. They painted the walls and hung up posters. "Can you help us to carry the desk upstairs?" the girls asked Dad. "I'm coming," he answered. "Would you all like to have a cup of tea?" Mrs. Miller called.

35. Complete the sentences as in the example.

Example: A secretary is *a person who types letters*.
a) An ambulance is a vehicle which takes injured people to hospital
b) A nurse is a person who looks after people who are ill.

36. Put the parts of the sentences in the correct order.

a) your / last year / did / holiday / enjoy / you / ?
Did you enjoy your holiday last year
b) doesn't / early / getting up / he / in the morning / like / ,
he doesn't like getting up early in the morning

37. Put the parts of these sentences into the correct order.

a) Mary's birthday / bought / for / a present / have / already / you
Have you already bought a present for Mary's birthday?
b) buy / but / tomorrow / a watch / I'm / her / going to / no
No,

Übungsaufgaben: Language Test

38. Put the parts of these sentences in the correct order.

a) your holidays / you / where / going / this summer / are / to spend

Where _are you going to spend your holidays this summer_?

b) the mountains / I want / this year / Bavaria / in the south of / and lakes / to visit

This year _I want to visit the mountains and lakes in the south of Bavaria_.

c) in the north / to see / some places / don't / forget / too

Don't _forget to see some places in the north, too_.

39. What do you say in the following situations?

a) Sage, dass du in Ruhe gelassen werden willst, weil du Kopfschmerzen hast.

Leave me along because I have

b) Dein Freund hat sich entschuldigt, weil er versehentlich deinen Stift benutzt hat. Du sagst, dass es dir nichts ausmacht.

c) Sage, dass du nicht gerne früh aufstehst.

d) Du sitzt im Wartezimmer einer Arztpraxis. Die Luft ist sehr schlecht. Frage höflich, ob du das Fenster öffnen darfst.

e) Sage, dass CDs teurer als Kassetten sind.

40. Say it in English.

a) Frage deinen Freund, was er am Wochenende gemacht hat.

b) Sage, dass du vorhast, im nächsten Sommer nach Irland zu fahren.

c) Stelle fest, dass die U-Bahn schneller als der Bus ist.

d) Sage, dass du nicht gerne zum Zahnarzt gehst.

e) (Dein englischer Freund ist der Meinung, dass Tanzen Spaß macht.) Stimme zu.

41. Was sagt man in folgenden Situationen?

a) Schlage vor, eine Pizza zu essen.

b) Die Verkäuferin fragt, ob die Jeans passen.

c) Sage, dass du froh bist, eine Lehrstelle zu haben.

d) Bestelle in einem Café ein Stück Kuchen und eine Tasse Kaffee.

e) Frage deinen Freund, was er von Bungee-Jumping hält.

42. Was sagst du in folgenden Situationen?

a) Bitte jemanden, dir einen Regenschirm zu leihen.

b) (Jemand bedankt sich.) Du erwiderst „Bitte schön".

c) Frage deinen Freund, ob er seine Jeans selbst bezahlen muss.

d) (Jemand wünscht dir einen schönen Tag.) Du wünschst ihm dasselbe.

e) Die Verkäuferin fragt die Kundin, wonach sie sucht.

f) Frage, wo man hier die billigsten CDs kaufen kann.

43. Was sagst du in folgenden Situationen?

a) Du bist in London. Frage einen Passanten höflich nach dem Weg zur Tower Bridge.

b) Der Engländer spricht sehr schnell. Sage ihm, dass du ihn nicht verstanden hast.

c) Nach der Besichtigung der Tower Bridge besuchst du ein Lokal. An einem Tisch sitzt ein englischer Junge. Frage ihn, ob du Platz nehmen darfst.

d) Ihr kommt ins Gespräch. Du erzählst ihm, dass du mit dem Zug nach Cambridge fahren willst.

e) Frage den englischen Jungen, ob er schon einmal in Cambridge war.

44. Was sagst du in folgenden Situationen?

a) Bitte deine Freundin, dir bei den Hausaufgaben zu helfen.

b) Frage, wann das nächste Schiff nach Dover abfährt.

c) Bedauere, dass du im Augenblick sehr beschäftigt bist.

d) Sage, dass du nicht viel Geld ausgeben möchtest.

45. Was sagst du in folgenden Situationen?

a) Bedauere, dass das Wetter so schlecht ist.

b) (Dein Freund möchte ins Schwimmbad gehen.) Mache einen Gegenvorschlag: Du willst ins Kino.

c) Bitte deine Freunde, in deinem Zimmer nicht zu rauchen.

d) Sage, dass deiner Meinung nach die Probe schwierig war.

e) Wünsche deiner Schwester einen schönen Urlaub.

f) Frage deinen Onkel, ob er sich für Tennis interessiert.

46. Was sagst du in folgenden Situationen am Bahnhof?

a) Frage den Schalterbeamten, wie lange die Fahrt nach Winchester dauert.

b) Sage ihm, dass du glaubst, dass der Fahrkartenautomat nicht funktioniert.

c) Frage den Schalterbeamten, ob er dir sagen kann, wo der Wartesaal ist.

d) Sage, dass du ihn nicht verstanden hast.

e) Sage deiner Freundin, dass es dir nichts ausmacht zu warten.

f) Sage, dass du einen Kaffee trinken wirst, wenn er nicht zu teuer ist.

47. Which word sounds different at the underlined place?

Example: sh<u>ou</u>ld – w<u>oo</u>d – sh<u>ou</u>t – w<u>ou</u>ld – g<u>oo</u>d

a) ch<u>i</u>ld – <u>until</u> – w<u>i</u>ld – n<u>i</u>ght – r<u>i</u>de

b) cl<u>ea</u>r – <u>ea</u>r – b<u>ea</u>r – d<u>ea</u>r – h<u>ea</u>r

c) m<u>o</u>ney – d<u>o</u>ne – s<u>o</u>n – g<u>o</u>ne – w<u>o</u>n

d) sch<u>oo</u>l – b<u>oo</u>t – f<u>oo</u>t – c<u>oo</u>l – f<u>oo</u>d

Reading Comprehension Text

Action on wheels

Here comes the big hill! Faster! Heart pounding, leg muscles ache. Jump! Sharp turn, then down the hill. Careful! Remember the last time! No, don't slow down! Watch out for the pebbles! Big side step! Keep your balance! Watch the traffic – a car is coming. Faster! Bang! Knee hits the pavement. Dirt in my mouth, the taste of blood. Why am I doing this?

Inline skating is more than just skating around in the neighbourhood, looking and talking to friends. Many people think it is the ideal sport. But what are its origins? Long before inline skates were invented, a primitive kind of roller skates was developed by a Dutchman about 200 years ago. Wanting to practise ice-skating during the summer, he fastened wooden spools[1] to the bottom of his shoes. Other inventions followed. In 1823 Robert John Tyers of London designed a skate called a "rolito" by putting four wheels in a line on the bottom of a shoe. This was the beginning of inline skates, but they didn't become popular at that time.

One day in 1980 two brothers from Minneapolis found an old inline skate. Scott and Brennan Olson were ice hockey players, and they realized that inline skates could be used for their summer training. So they redesigned the skate and added some things like a rubber heel brake. Soon after that they began selling skates out of their home, and inline skating was reborn. The Olsons didn't foresee that it would not only become a new sport but would even create a new lifestyle.

Is inline skating really the ideal sport? Why would anyone want to do something like this? Few other sports offer so much variety and excitement, and it's much more fun than doing exercises in a health club. You only need a pair of inline skates, elbow and knee pads, gloves and a helmet. And you can go skating anywhere – in the street, in a car park or even up and down a stairway. You can skate just for fun or skate freestyle, do stunt-skating or dance-skating, play hockey or anything else you can imagine. Whether you do it alone or with friends, you can have a good time and get in shape, too.

Inline skating helps you test your body's limits and is also good training for other sports. It's easy to learn, and people of all ages can do it, but it can be dangerous and skaters shouldn't be too aggressive. Watch out for your own safety but also for other people around you. Many inline skaters risk their own health and endanger other people by crashing into pedestrians, cyclists or cars. Still, inline skating is a very popular sport for everyone. Even famous actors like Dustin Hoffman and Robert De Niro do it. It was reported that, when they were skating in Central Park recently, they couldn't brake in time to stop. Their uncontrolled style of skating frightened two police horses, which then threw off their riders into a duck pond.

1 spool: Fadenrolle

1. Answer the questions. Give short answers.

a) Where does the word "inline skate" come from?

_____

b) When did the Olsons come across an old inline skate?

_____

c) How did the Olson brothers improve the design of inline skates?

_____

d) What should inline skaters wear for their safety?

_____

e) Who frightened two police horses?

_____

2. **Write down the line numbers. Find the expression from the text which tells you ...**

   a) ... that roller skates are older than inline skates.

   Lines: _____

   b) ... that inline skates were not successful at first.

   Lines: _____

   c) ... why the Olson brothers redesigned the old inline skate.

   Lines: _____

   d) ... that you can do different sporting activities on inline skates.

   Lines: _____

3. **Form four sentences that fit the text.**

   Use each part of the sentence only once.

Inline skating is not only a popular sport	whether	they endanger their own and other people's health.
You can skate alone	although	a new kind of lifestyle, too.
More and more teenagers skate aggressively	because	it's good training for other sports.
Lots of people do inline skating	but	together with friends.
	or	it's good training for other sports.

   a) _____
   b) _____
   c) _____
   d) _____

Abschlussprüfungen an Hauptschulen in Bayern – Englisch
Übungsaufgaben: Text Production

Letter – Brieffreund in Dallas

Beachte: Dein Brief sollte mindestens 10 Sätze umfassen.
Denke an die Briefform (Datum, Anrede, Grußformel).

Angaben zum Briefempfänger:
Steve, dein Brieffreund, ist 16 Jahre alt. Er lebt in Dallas und hat dir in seinem letzten Brief über seinen Besuch in New York geschrieben. Du hast vor kurzem vier Tage mit deinen Eltern in London verbracht und berichtest nun deinem amerikanischen Brieffreund darüber.

Angaben zum Briefinhalt:
- Bedanke dich für Steves letzten Brief.
- Berichte, dass du vor einigen Wochen mit deinen Eltern vier Tage in London verbracht hast.
- Sage, dass ihr ein Hotel in der Nähe des Hyde Parks hattet. Es war sehr teuer und ihr musstet für das Frühstück extra bezahlen. Die Zimmer waren ziemlich schmutzig.
- Deine Eltern wollten Sehenswürdigkeiten besichtigen. Sie besuchten z. B. ...
- Du bist nicht mitgegangen. Aber du hast dir ein U-Bahn-Ticket für drei Tage gekauft.
- Sage, dass du das Hard Rock Café gesucht und wirklich gefunden hast. Du hast dort ein weiteres T-Shirt mit dem Zeichen „Hard Rock Café" gekauft, weil du sie sammelst.
- Es war großartig, dass du im Hard Rock Café einige nette Engländer kennen gelernt hast und ihr viel Spaß hattet.
- Berichte, dass du dann zu einem Straßenmarkt gingst.
  Du hast ... (z. B. CDs, eine Playstation, Sweatshirts) für einen guten Preis bekommen.
- Frage Steve, ob er schon in London war.
- Sage, dass es eine sehr aufregende Stadt ist.
- Schreibe, dass du dich auf Steves Antwort freust.

Picture Story: Late for dinner

Look at the pictures and tell the story in at least 10 sentences. You can start like this:

Late for dinner
On a nice weekend in July two brothers, Sammy and Henry, and their dog Scottie went on a camping trip in the Scottish Highlands.
After a long hiking-tour …

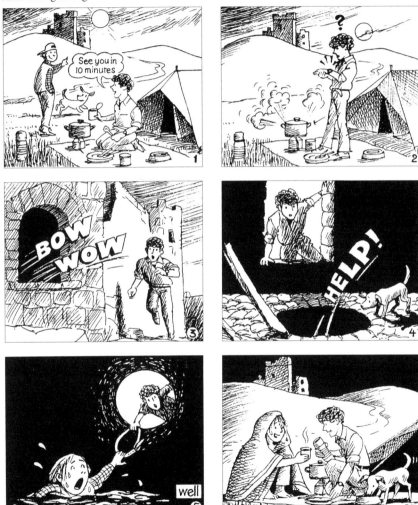

Abschlussprüfungen an Hauptschulen in Bayern – Englisch
Übungsaufgaben: Mündliche Prüfung

Oral Report

J. K. Rowling

Bereite ein Referat über J. K. Rowling, die Autorin der Harry-Potter-Bücher vor.

Expressive Reading

Crime in South Africa

Read the text aloud.

Crime has become one of the biggest problems in South Africa. * The rich, white people have moved into safe areas outside of the big cities. Anyone who can pay for it has put up walls around their homes or moved into "compounds". A compound is made up of some houses which have one wall around them and a gate. Anyone who wants to go into the compound has to talk to the guard at the gate. Before allowing any visitors inside, the guard will call the person who lives there by phone, to check if he or she is at home. * Many houses are like castles: the windows have bars in them and the doors are very strong. Still, the homes of the rich are robbed quite often. The criminals will wait for the houseowner to come home at night, and then force him to open the door. Or they will attack the guard of a compound with guns to get inside. Of course, it is most dangerous for women to come home at night alone. * But just driving a car has also become very dangerous. When a driver stops at a red traffic light, it can happen that a criminal comes up to the car with a gun in his hand and forces the driver to open his window. In that situation, it is best to give the criminal what he wants.

Tipps:
– Lege kurze Sprechpausen ein, wo es sinnvoll ist (mögliche Pausen sind mit * markiert).
– Achte auf die Aussprache. Sollte ein Wort vorkommen, das dir vielleicht nocht nicht bekannt ist, reagiere nicht verunsichert. Ziehe Parallelen zur Aussprache anderer Wörter, z. B.: „compound" [ˈkɔmpaʊnd]: bekannt ist die Aussprache von „com" (wie in „computer"), sowie „pound" (wie „£").

Guided Dialogue

In a hotel

Form English sentences. Use the information given in German. Do not translate word by word.

You're in New York with your boyfriend/girlfriend. You've just arrived at the hotel.

RECEPTIONIST: Good afternoon. What can I do for you?

YOU: Grüße. Sage, wie dein Name ist, und dass du eine Reservierung gemacht hast.

RECEPTIONIST: Mr./Mrs./Ms. ... Your reservation is from 15th to 18th August. The checkout time is 10 a.m. Do you want a king-sized bed or two twin beds?

YOU: Sage, dass ihr getrennte Betten nehmt. Frage, ob es im Zimmer ein Bad und einen Fernseher gibt.

RECEPTIONIST: Yes, of course. There's a bathroom with a shower. You'll also find a minibar in your room. Could I have your credit card, please?

YOU: Du überreichst deine Kreditkarte. Frage, ob sie euch um 6:00 Uhr morgens aufwecken könnten. Ihr werdet die Freiheitsstatue auf Liberty Island besichtigen.

RECEPTIONIST: Sure! We'll give you a wake-up-call. Here's your key. Your room number is 223. It's on the second floor.

YOU: Frage, wo es Frühstück gibt, und ob man es extra bezahlen muss.

RECEPTIONIST: We serve breakfast from 6 to 10 a.m. The breakfast room is on the first floor. Breakfast is included.

YOU: Frage, ob ihr im Hotel Karten für das Broadway Musical „Lion King" kaufen könnt und wie viel die billigsten Karten kosten.

RECEPTIONIST: Sorry. We don't sell theatre tickets. You can buy them at the theatres on Broadway or at the ticket office on Times Square.

YOU: Bedanke dich für die Hilfe und verabschiede dich.

Lösungen zu den Übungsaufgaben

Listening Comprehension Test: E-mail from Munich

1. **Underline the right word.**
   a) Nicole misses the English TV programmes/<u>weather</u>/food.
   b) Being an exchange student is <u>interesting</u>/intelligent/difficult.
   c) Nicole/<u>Katja</u>/Katja's father is ill.
   d) Julia lived in the UK/United Emirates/<u>US</u> when she was younger.
   e) It's hard to follow the lessons in sports/maths/<u>history</u>.
   f) Julia is having a picnic/<u>party</u>/tour next Friday.
   g) During their trip to Munich, Nicole visited a <u>church</u>/a soccer match/a rock concert.
   h) At the end of the tour they went <u>shopping</u>/to Neuschwanstein/to the country.

2. **One ending is correct for each of the following sentences. Tick it (✓).**

   a) Nicole has been in Munich
   - ☐ for a month.
   - ☑ for a week.
   - ☐ four weeks.

   b) Katja
   - ☑ isn't good at English.
   - ☐ isn't good at school.
   - ☐ isn't German.

   c) The best English is spoken by
   - ☑ Julia.
   - ☐ Katja.
   - ☐ the sports teacher.

   d) Nicole tries to speak
   - ☐ dialect.
   - ☐ a little German.
   - ☑ a lot of German.

   e) The Olympic Games were held in Munich in
   - ☐ 1970.
   - ☑ 1972.
   - ☐ 1927.

Language Test

1. **Look at the label.**

   a) telephone b) stove
   c) blanket d) socks

2. **Cross out the word that doesn't fit.**

   a) skin b) plate
   c) boot d) flour

3. **Find one more example and the collective noun.**

   a) gold, iron, bronze, …: metal(s)/mineral(s)
   b) hammer, axe, pair of pliers, …: tool(s)
   c) snow, clouds, wind, …: weather

4. **Give two examples for each collective noun.**

   a) vegetables: beans, peas, corn („Mais"), carrots, cucumber („Gurke") …

   b) desserts: muffin, cake, apple-pie, fruit, …

   c) meat: duck („Ente"), turkey („Putenfleisch"), pork („Schweinefleisch"), beef („Rindfleisch"), veal („Kalbfleisch"), poultry („Geflügel"), chicken („Hähnchenfleisch"), lamb („Lammfleisch"), mutton („Hammelfleisch"), venison („Wildbret")

5. **Cross out the word that doesn't fit and find the collective noun.**

   a) ~~pears~~ → vegetables
   b) ~~watch~~ → clothes
   c) ~~food~~ → (parts of the) body

6. **What do you need to …**

   a) knife/bread knife b) washing machine/washing powder
   c) key d) (electric) toothbrush, toothpaste

7. **Where can you find these persons and things?**

   a) airport
   b) hotel/guest house/motel

c) garage/petrol station/filling station
   d) beach/seaside

8. **Where do people usually do that?**

   a) university/college
   b) bank
   c) airport
   d) (car) factory
   e) police (station)
   f) fridge/cooler

9. **Name one thing in each sentence.**

   a) countries/rivers/mountains/our planet/continents ...

   b) wars/(famous) people/queens/kings/famous events ...

   c) nature/animals/the human being/plants/insects ...

   d) the law/civil rights/our city/our town/our village/government ...

10. **In what countries are these languages spoken?**

    a) France
    b) Holland/the Netherlands
    c) Greece
    d) Norway

11. **Find another word with the same meaning.**

    a) difficult
    b) happy/pleased
    c) finish/be over
    d) present

12. **Find the opposites.**

    a) terrible/dreadful/awful/very bad
    b) healthy/fit
    c) different
    d) earns/makes

13. **Find the opposites of the underlined words.**

    a) hard/difficult
    b) catch
    c) spend/waste
    d) cry/be sad

14. **Write down the feminine form.**

    a) daughter
    b) queen
    c) wife
    d) waitress

15. Put the following words into the plural form.

a) mice
b) children
c) ladies
d) knives

16. Find the adjectives.

a) healthy
b) beautiful
c) dangerous
d) active

17. Fill in the right preposition. What has the police dog got to do?

a) over
b) under
c) through
d) across

18. Fill in the right preposition.

Hinweis: Die folgenden Verhältniswörter kommen in festen Verbindungen vor. Da es keine Regel gibt, solltest du sie lernen (z. B. zur Schule gehen – „to go <u>to</u> school").

a) between („zwischen")
b) to/in
c) from
d) about/of

19. Choose the right word for the questions.

a) Who …
b) What …
c) When …
d) How many …
e) Which …
f) How much …

20. Fill in the missing words.

Hinweis: Manchmal entsprechen einem deutschen Zeitwort mehrere englische Zeitwörter, z. B.: ein Hemd tragen – „to <u>wear</u> a shirt", einen Koffer tragen – „to <u>carry</u> a suitcase".

a) carry
b) ride
c) sweet
d) (shop) assistant/salesperson

21. Choose the right verbs.

"I'm going to **wear** my blue dress. I'm sure my friends would like to **listen** to the latest Hip Hop CD. Perhaps we'll **watch** a video on TV, too. I'm going to **tell** my friends some jokes as well. After the party my friends will **ride/get** home on their bikes. I wonder what presents I will **get**."

22. Fill in the right verb.

a) broke b) was
c) bought d) wrote

23. Put the verbs in brackets into the simple past.

invited – put on – ate – drank – took – felt

24. Fill in the infinitive forms of the verbs.

ride – drive – catch – feed – throw – build

25. Find the correct ending to each sentence.

a) 2: At the moment Mr Jones is visiting a conference in New York.

b) 3: Two years ago he slept in his car because he couldn't get a room in a hotel.

c) 4: Tomorrow he will watch a musical on Broadway. *oder*
2: Tomorrow Mr Jones is visiting a conference in New York.

d) 1: Every morning he jogs in Central Park.

26. Fill in the correct forms of the verbs.

flew, 'll (I will) visit/I'm going to visit/I'm visiting, Have, been, sounds

27. Fill in the correct forms of the verbs.

a) was b) takes
c) will buy/is going to buy/is buying d) have already seen

28. Mark the right meaning with a cross.

a) She listens to the radio and does her homework at the same time.

b) She is going to buy a stereo.

c) Sally did her homework first.

29. Make negative sentences.

a) … doesn't like …
b) … didn't buy …
c) … will not go/won't go/(I)'m not going/won't be going

30. Ask questions.

a) Where did you stay?
b) What was the weather like?
c) How much/What did it cost?

31. Ask the question.

Where are you from? / Where do you come from?

How long have you been here?

Did you like | the show?
       enjoy | the parade?
             | it?

What are you going to do next? / What are you planning to do next?

32. Find the right form.

a) nicer than
b) as loud as
c) the most beautiful

33. Finish these sentences.

a) If it's warm next Sunday, we'll go swimming.
b) If it rains, we'll stay at home.

34. Fill in the right pronouns.

The Millers moved to a new house because **their** flat had become too small. Mary and **her** sister Jane got a big room on the first floor. **They** painted the walls and hung up posters. "Can you help **us** to carry the desk upstairs?" the girls asked Dad. "I'm coming," **he** answered. "Would **you/we** all like to have a cup of tea?" Mrs. Miller called.

35. Complete the sentences as in the example.

a) An ambulance is a vehicle which/that takes injured people to hospital.
b) A nurse is a person who looks after people who are ill.

36. Put the parts of the sentences in the correct order.

a) Did you enjoy your holiday last year?

b) He doesn't like getting up early in the morning.

37. Put the parts of these sentences into the correct order.

a) Have you already bought a present for Mary's birthday?

b) No, but I'm going to buy her a watch tomorrow.
No, but tomorrow I'm going to buy her a watch.

38. Put the parts of these sentences in the correct order.

a) Where are you going to spend your holidays this summer?

b) This year I want to visit the mountains and lakes in the south of Bavaria. /
I want to visit the mountains and lakes in the south of Bavaria this year.

c) Don't forget to see some places in the north, too.

39. What do you say in the following situations?

a) Please leave me alone. I've got a headache.

b) That's okay.
I don't mind.

c) I don't like getting up early in the morning.

d) May/Could I open the window?
Would you mind if I opened the window?

e) CDs are more expensive than cassettes.

40. Say it in English.

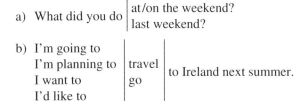

d) I don't like | going | to the dentist.
   I hate | to go |

e) I think so too.
   I agree.
   You're right.

41. Was sagt man in folgenden Situationen?

a) Let's | eat | a pizza.
         | have |
   What about having a pizza?
   What about a pizza?

b) Do the/those jeans fit?
   Are the/those jeans | okay?
                      | the right size?

c) I'm glad I've got an apprenticeship.

d) Can I have | (a piece of) cake and (a cup of) coffee, please?
   I'd like | (a piece of) cake and (a cup of) coffee, please.
   I'll have |
   Coffee and cake, please.

e) What do you think | of | bungee-jumping?
                     | about |

42. Was sagst du in folgenden Situationen?

a) Could | I borrow | an | umbrella, please?
   Can | you lend me | your |

b) Don't mention it
   You're welcome.
   Not at all.

c) Do you have to | pay for your jeans yourself?
   Have you got to |

d) Thank you! (The) same to you.
   Thank you! You too.

e) What are you looking for?
   Can I help you?
   How may/can I help you?

f) Where can | I / you | buy / get | the cheapest CDs here?

43. Was sagst du in folgenden Situationen?

a) Excuse me, | could you tell me the way to / do you know the way to / can you tell me the way to | Tower Bridge, (please)?

b) Sorry, / Pardon, | I didn't understand you.

c) Excuse me, | is there anybody sitting here? / can I sit here? / is this seat taken/free? / do you mind if I sit here?

d) I want / I'd like | to go to Cambridge by train.
   I'm going (to go) to Cambridge by train.

e) Have you ever been to Cambridge?

44. Was sagst du in folgenden Situationen?

a) Would you / Could you / Can you | help me with my homework, please?
   Please help me with my homework!
   Will you help me with my homework?

b) When | does / will | the next | ship / ferry | to Dover | leave? / go?
   When will the next ferry be leaving?
   When is the next ship to Dover?

c) Sorry, (but) I'm | very / so | busy | at the moment. / now.
   I'm afraid I've got a lot to do | at the moment. / right now.

d) I don't want to
   I'm not going to | spend | much / a lot of / a large amount of | money.
   I don't intend to
   I won't

45. Was sagst du in folgenden Situationen?

a) What a pity / It's a shame | (that) the weather is so bad.
   I wish the weather weren't so bad.

b) How / What | about going to the cinema?
   Why don't we go to the cinema?

   I'd rather
   I'd prefer to | go to the cinema.
   Let's

c) Please don't smoke in my room.
   (If you don't mind,) I'd rather you didn't smoke in my room.
   Would you mind not smoking in my room?

d) In my opinion the test was | difficult.
   I thought the test was | hard.

e) Have a nice holiday.
   Have a good time.
   Enjoy your holiday.

f) Are you interested in tennis?
   Do you like tennis?

46. Was sagst du in folgenden Situationen am Bahnhof?

a) How long does the | journey / trip / train-ride / train | to Winchester take? / take to Winchester?
   How long does it take to get to Winchester?
   How long does it take to Winchester?

b) I guess / I'm afraid | (that) the ticket-machine | is out of order. / is broken. / doesn't work. / isn't working.

I think (that) the ticket-machine | is out of order.
                                  | is broken.
I don't think (that) the ticket-machine is working.

c) Can
   Could | you tell me where the waiting-room is?
   Would
   Where's the waiting-room, please?

d) Excuse me, | I didn't | get you.
   Sorry, | | understand (you).
              | | quite catch that.
   I'm sorry, what did you say?
   Pardon, what did you say?
   Could you repeat what you just said?

e) I don't mind | waiting
                | having to wait.
   It doesn't matter if I/we have to wait.
   It's no problem for me to wait.

f) I'll | have | | it's not too expensive.
   I'm going to| get | a (cup of) coffee if | it isn't too expensive.
               | buy | | it doesn't cost too much.
               | order | | it's not too dear.

47. Which word sounds different at the underlined place?

   a) ch<u>i</u>ld – un<s>til</s> – w<u>i</u>ld – n<u>ig</u>ht – r<u>i</u>de

   b) cl<u>ea</u>r – <u>ea</u>r – <s>bear</s> – d<u>ea</u>r – h<u>ea</u>r

   c) m<u>o</u>ney – d<u>o</u>ne – s<u>o</u>n – <s>gone</s> – w<u>o</u>n

   d) sch<u>oo</u>l – b<u>oo</u>t – <s>foot</s> – c<u>oo</u>l – f<u>oo</u>d

Reading Comprehension Test: Action on wheels

1. **Answer the questions. Give short answers.**
   a) From the wheels that are in a line (on the bottom of a shoe). (Z. 24/25)
   b) (One day) in 1980. (Z. 29/30)
   c) They added some things like a rubber heel brake. (Z. 33/34)
   d) (They should wear) elbow and knee pads, gloves and a helmet. (Z. 43/44)
   e) Dustin Hoffman and Robert De Niro (on inline skates). (Z. 61–66)

2. **Write down the line numbers. Find the expression from the text which tells you ...**
   a) Lines 19–21 ("Long before inline skates were invented, a primitive kind of roller skates was developed by a Dutchman about 200 years ago.")
   b) Lines 27/28 ("... but they didn't become popular at that time.")
   c) Lines 30–33 ("Scott and Brennan Olson were ice hockey players, and they realized that inline skates could be used for their summer training.")
   d) Lines 46–49 ("You can skate just for fun or skate freestyle, do stunt-skating or dance-skating, play hockey or anything else you can imagine.")

3. **Form four sentences that fit the text.**
   a) Inline skating is not only a popular sport but a new kind of lifestyle, too.
   b) You can skate alone or together with friends.
   c) More and more teenagers skate aggressively although they endanger their own and other people's health.
   d) Lots of people do inline skating because it's good training for other sports.

Text Production: Letter

Dear Steve, 24/06/04[1]

Thank you very much for your last letter. (You told me a lot of interesting things about New York and I'd also like to go there one day!)
Some weeks ago my parents and I spent four days in London. Our hotel was near Hyde Park. It was very expensive but we still[2] had to pay extra for breakfast. The rooms weren't very nice either – they were rather dirty.
My parents wanted to do a lot of sightseeing. They visited Buckingham Palace, the Tower of London and Madame Tussaud's. They didn't see the Queen at Buckingham Palace, only some guards. But they met a lot of "stars" at Madame Tussaud's. (It's a really cool museum.) It's a pity[3] I didn't go with them.
I bought a three-day ticket for the underground – the Tube. That's what the Londoners call their subway. I looked for the Hard Rock Cafe, because I'm a real fan and also collect the T-shirts. I really found it! It was great to meet some English kids there, and we had a lot of fun together!
Then I visited a street market that was very, very big. I bought some CDs and even got[4] a playstation at a very good price.
Have you ever been to London? It's a very exciting city!!!
I'm looking forward to your next letter!

Lots of love

Vanessa

1 *oder:* June 24th, 2004
2 *still*: dennoch
3 *it's a pity:* es ist schade
4 *to get, got, got:* bekommen

Text Production: Picture Story

Late for dinner

On a nice weekend in July two brothers, Sammy and Henry, and their dog Scottie[1] went on a camping trip in the Scottish Highlands. After a long hiking-tour they put up their tent for the night near an[2] old castle. While Henry started to cook dinner on a camping stove, Sammy wanted to take a quick look at the castle. "I'll be back in ten minutes", he said. He and Scottie went up the hill[3] to the castle. After ten minutes the meal was ready and the sun started to set[4], but Sammy and the dog didn't return. Henry was really nervous now and decided[5] to look for[6] his brother. He ran up the hill and heard Scottie barking loudly[7]. The sound was coming out of a window in the old castle. Henry got inside and saw the dog near a well in the old floor.

Sammy had fallen into the well[8] and was shouting, "Henry, help me, help me!" The well wasn't very deep but it was full of water and Sammy wasn't able to get out himself. Henry had a good idea: he took the belt[9] of his trousers and held it in the hole so that his brother could hold on to it while he pulled him out.

Henry, Sammy and Scottie went back to their tent and Sammy wrapped[10] himself in a blanket[11] to warm up again. He was very happy, and said to his brother, "Thanks for your help and the hot dinner!"

1   vorgegebene Namen beachten
2   „a" wird zu „an", wenn der nächste Wortbeginn mit einem Selbstlaut ausgesprochen wird
3   *hill:* Hügel
4   *to set:* untergehen
5   *to decide:* sich entscheiden
6   *to look for:* suchen nach
7   *loudly:* Adverb zu „loud" (Wie bellte der Hund? – laut)
8   *well:* Brunnen
9   *belt:* Gürtel
10 *to wrap:* einwickeln
11 *blanket:* Decke

Mündliche Prüfung: Oral Report

Beispielreferat zu J. K. Rowling

Like many people, I am a great fan of Harry Potter. I have read all of the Harry Potter books and seen the films in the cinema. Today I would like to tell you a few things about the person who invented Harry Potter, the British author Joanne Kathleen Rowling.

Better known as J. K. Rowling, she was born in Chipping Sodbury, England in 1965. She grew up in a town called Chepstow and then went to study French at Exeter University. As a student, she also spent a year in Paris. Later, J. K. Rowling moved to London to work for the human rights organization[1] Amnesty International. J. K. Rowling had the idea of Harry Potter while she was riding on a train from Manchester to London in 1990, and started to write the first book. Because she did not earn any money as an author at that time, she could only write in her free time. J. K. Rowling studied to become a teacher and moved to Portugal, where she taught English. She got married and had a baby. But later she had to raise[2] the child by herself. Sometimes she was only able to write the Harry Potter book when her little daughter was sleeping.

Before publishing[3] the first book, J. K. Rowling had very little money. While she was still studying to become a teacher, she and her baby had to live on 70 pounds a week. She was very glad when a female friend helped her and lent[4] her 4000 pounds. After she became rich, J. K. Rowling bought that friend a flat in Edinburgh.

"Harry Potter and the Philosopher's Stone" was finally published in 1997 and was a great success[5]. Before that, most children had only been interested in television or computer games, but then they started to read again. But it was not just children, who liked Harry Potter – their parents did too. The next Harry Potter books followed quickly, and the films came into the cinemas. J. K. Rowling became one of the best-selling authors in the world. The third book, "Harry Potter and the Goblet of Fire", was sold three million times in the first 48 hours after the sales[6] started. It is the "fastest selling book in history". You can buy Harry Potter books in 200 countries and in 61 languages.

J. K. Rowling has won many international prizes for her books and become very rich. In 2004, she has over 500 million pounds. Today she lives in Scotland with her husband and two children. I hope that she will continue to write Harry Potter books!

1 *human rights organization:* Menschenrechtsorganisation
2 *to raise:* aufziehen
3 *to publish:* veröffentlichen
4 *to lend:* leihen
5 *success:* Erfolg
6 *sale:* Verkauf

Mündliche Prüfung: Guided Dialogue

In a hotel

Hinweis: Auch andere Lösungen sind möglich.

RECEPTIONIST: Good afternoon. What can I do for you?
YOU: Hello, my name is … I've made a reservation.
RECEPTIONIST: Mr./Mrs./Ms. … Your reservation is from 15th to 18th August. The checkout time is 10 a.m. Do you want a king-sized bed or two twin beds?
YOU: We'd like to have twin beds. Is there a bathroom and a TV in the room?
RECEPTIONIST: Yes, of course. There's a bathroom with a shower. You'll also find a minibar in your room. Could I have your credit card, please?
YOU: Here you are. Could you please wake us up at 6 o'clock in the morning? We are going to see the Statue of Liberty on Liberty Island.

RECEPTIONIST: Sure! We'll give you a wake-up-call. Here's your key. Your room number is 223. It's on the second floor.
YOU: Where can we eat breakfast? Do we have to pay extra for it?
RECEPTIONIST: We serve breakfast from 6 to 10 a.m. The breakfast room is on the first floor. Breakfast is included.
YOU: Can we buy tickets for the musical "Lion King" at the hotel? How much do the cheapest tickets cost? / How much are the cheapest tickets?
RECEPTIONIST: Sorry. We don't sell theatre tickets. You can buy them at the theatres on Broadway or at the ticket office on Times Square.
YOU: Thanks for your help. Goodbye.

Schriftliche Abschlussprüfungsaufgaben

Bildnachweis
James Moore

> Abschlussprüfung an Hauptschulen in Bayern
> Englisch Übungsaufgabe im Stil des Quali

Listening Comprehension Text

Flight 175

Good morning, ladies and gentlemen. This is your captain speaking. My name is Sandy Brown and I'd like to welcome you aboard on flight 175 from Hannover to London Heathrow[1].

I'm sorry to tell you that our flight will start 20 minutes later than scheduled[2], as the airspace[3] over southern Britain is overcrowded[4] at the moment. Our flight will take one hour, so we will land at Heathrow Airport at about three thirty. We will be flying at an altitude of 35,000 feet and our average speed[5] will be 600 miles per hour. We should be crossing the Channel at about ten past three. The weather in London is nice and sunny, with temperatures at about 25 degrees Celsius[6].

I hope you have a pleasant flight and that you enjoy your stay in London. Thank you for flying with British Airways. I'm looking forward to seeing you again on board one of our flights.

Vokabeln
1 Heathrow – *Flughafen in London*
2 scheduled – *planmäßig*
3 airspace – *Luftraum*
4 overcrowded – *überfüllt*
5 average speed – *durchschnittliche Geschwindigkeit*
6 degree Celsius – *Grad Celsius*

Übungsaufgabe im Stil des Quali

A Listening Comprehension Test

1. **Listen to the CD and tick (✓) what is right.**

		true	false
a)	The captain's name is Susan Brown.	☐	✓
b)	She welcomes the passengers aboard flight 157 from Hannover to London Heathrow.	☐	✓
c)	The flight will start 20 minutes later than scheduled.	✓	☐
d)	The airspace over southern Britain is not overcrowded.	☐	✓
e)	The flight will take one hour.	✓	☐
f)	They will be flying at an altitude of 25,000 feet.	☐	✓
g)	Their average speed will be 600 miles per hour.	✓	☐
h)	The weather in London is rainy.	☐	✓
i)	Temperatures will be at about 25 degrees Fahrenheit.	☐	✓

2. **What describes the text you have heard the best?**

   ✓ It is an announcement *(Durchsage)* by a flight captain.

   ☐ It is a speech delivered *(vorgetragen)* by a stewardess.

   ☐ One of the passengers is trying to entertain the other passengers.

3. **Fill in the missing information.**

numbers	We will be flying with an altitude of 35000 feet.	Our flight will start 20 minutes later than scheduled.
names	This is your captain speaking. My name is Sandy Brown.	We will land at Heathrow Airport.
towns	I'd like to welcome you aboard on flight 175 from Hannover to London Heathrow.	I hope you have a pleasant flight and that you enjoy your stay in London.

B Use of English

1. What do you need to …?

Example: cut bread — a knife ✓
- a washing machine ☐
- a spoon ☐

a) send e-mails
- an envelope ☐
- a computer ✓
- a TV ☐

b) listen to CDs
- a radio ☐
- a stereo / CD-Player ✓
- a cassette recorder ☐

c) cool your drinks
- a fridge ✓
- a stove ☐
- an electric iron ☐

d) clean the floor
- a toaster ☐
- a vacuum cleaner ✓
- a microwave ☐

2. Which parts go together? Draw lines.

a)	May I	get	the window?
b)	I can	borrow	with my homework, please?
c)	Could I	open	an apprenticeship.
d)	I'm glad	help me	your pen, please?
e)	Would you	I've got	was difficult.
f)	In my opinion	the test	to school faster by bike.

Übungsaufgabe im Stil des Quali

3. **Find the opposites.**

   a) louder — quieter
   b) slow — fast
   c) poor — rich
   d) crowded — empty
   e) less — more
   f) (to) sell — buy
   g) stupid — clever
   h) safe — unsafe
   i) tall — short
   j) always — never
   k) expensive — cheap
   l) (to) arrive — leave

4. **Find words with the same meaning. Choose the correct synonyms.**
   Example: maybe – **perhaps**

   job – rock – small – (to) run – short – quick – shut the door – shore – come in – (to) call

   a) stone — rock
   b) little — small
   c) beach — shore
   d) Close the door! — shut the door
   e) fast — quick
   f) work — job
   g) (to) phone s. o. — (to) call

5. **Put the verbs in the will-form. Look at Emily's plans for the week.**

   a) Next week I'll buy (buy) a birthday present for my brother.
   b) I think I'll buy (buy) a concert ticket for him.
   c) I hope the weather will be (be) good at the weekend.
   d) Matt and I will go (go) to the gym sometime next week.

6. **In English, please! Imagine the following situations and find the correct English phrase. You only have to give the English expression for the German phrase that indicates what you would say.**

   a) Du sitzt mit deinen Freunden im Café.
      Du möchtest wissen, was sie am Wochenende gemacht haben.
      What did you do on the weekend?

b) Du telefonierst mit deiner besten Freundin.
   Du kommst nicht mit ins Kino, weil du krank bist.
   I'm not coming with you. I feel ill.

c) Dein Bus hat Verspätung. Du rufst deinen Freund an, mit dem du verabredet bist.
   Du wirst dich ein wenig verspäten.
   I'm sorry, but I will be a little late.

d) Auf einer Party: Deine Freundin sagt, ihr gefällt die Party.
   Stimme ihr zu.
   I agree

e) Nach der Schule:
   Schlage vor, ins Kino zu gehen.
   Let's go to the cinema

C Reading Comprehension Test

An e-mail from Anthony

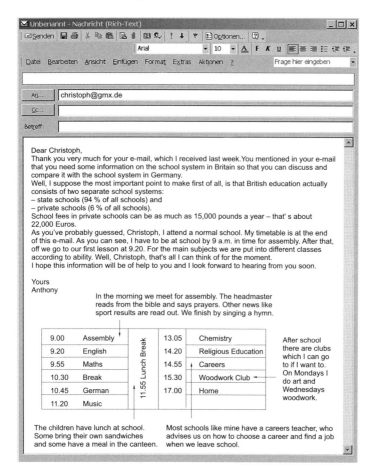

Vokabeln
mention	– erwähnen
suppose	– vermuten
school fee	– Schulgeld
probably	– wahrscheinlich
(to) guess	– raten, erraten
assembly	– morgendliche Versammlung an britischen Schulen
(to) advise	– hier: beraten

1. **Tick (✓) the right answer to each question.**

   a) Who received an e-mail last week?
   - ☐ Paul
   - ☑ Anthony
   - ☐ Christoph

   b) How much can school fees in private schools be?
   - ☑ 15,000 pounds
   - ☐ 6 % of the family income
   - ☐ 22,000 pounds

   c) What kind of school does Anthony go to?
   - ☑ state school
   - ☐ private school
   - ☐ no school at all

   d) When does Anthony have to be at school in the morning?
   - ☐ between 9 and 9.20 a.m.
   - ☐ at 9.20 a.m.
   - ☑ at 9 a.m.

   e) Where do the children have lunch?
   - ☐ at home
   - ☑ at school
   - ☐ at a restaurant

   f) When does Anthony attend which club?
   - ☑ art on Monday, woodwork on Wednesday
   - ☐ woodwork on Friday, art on Wednesday
   - ☐ woodwork on Monday, art on Wednesday

2. **The British school system. Read the dialogue between Christopher and his English teacher. Fill in the missing parts. You don't need all of the parts given.**

> your e-mail – yet – Have a nice day – your presentation – I'm looking forward – the preparation – in the afternoon – nice and sunny weather – about the British school system – German system – alright – he did – I agree

MR RYANT: "Did your friend from England answer _yet_?"

CHRISTOPHER: "Yes _he did_. In his e-mail he gave me a lot of information _about the British school system_."

MR RYANT: "That sounds good. Then you can do _your presentation_ on the British and German school system soon, can't you?"

CHRISTOPHER: "Yes of course. I started with _the preparation_ yesterday. I think I will be able to do it next Tuesday. Is that _alright_ with you?"

MR RYANT: "Of course it is. _I'm looking forward_ to your presentation. What do you think about the British school system in comparison to the _German system_?"

CHRISTOPHER: "What I most liked is that there are a lot of clubs _in the afternoon_ you can join. But "assembly" sounds a bit strange to me."

MR RYANT: "I can imagine that. _Have a nice day_ Christopher and good luck with your presentation."

CHRISTOPHER: "Thank you Mr Ryant. Bye."

3. **Answer the following questions in English.**

   a) Why does Christoph need information about British schools?

   _____
   _____

   b) Which basic facts do you learn about the British school system?

   _____
   _____

c) What happens during assembly? Mention three details.

d) What kind of subject is "Careers"?

D Text Production

Choose either 1. Picture Story or 2. Letter.

1. Picture Story

Write about 12–15 sentences. Try to describe things well.

(1) (2)

Konzert – Lieblingsband ausverkauft – enttäuscht

(3) (4)

Zeitung – Gewinnspiel gebrochenes Bein – verschenkt Tickets

(5)    (6)

auch zwei Tickets gewonnen   mit Freunden Konzert

2. Letter

Deine Tante und dein Onkel haben eine Wochenendreise nach Cambridge gemacht. Das Hotel war leider in einem furchtbaren Zustand: Das Zimmer war schmutzig, das Bett war kaputt und das Essen war ungenießbar. Leider ist das Englisch deiner Verwandten nicht so gut und so bitten sie dich, einen Beschwerdebrief an das Hotel zu verfassen. Die Notizen können dir helfen, den Brief zu schreiben:
- angemessene Anrede
- Adresse des Hotels: Europe Hotel, 24 Western Street, Cambridge, CB1 5NH, GB
- Layout des Briefes
- Liste die Mängel auf, über die deine Tante und dein Onkel sich beschweren möchten.
- Deine Tante und dein Onkel möchten einen Teil ihres Geldes zurückbekommen, weil der Zustand des Hotels so schlecht war.
- angemessene Verabschiedung

Übungsaufgabe im Stil des Quali

Lösungen

A   Listening Comprehension Test

1. Listen to the CD and tick (✓) what is right.

		true	false
a)	The captain's name is Susan Brown.	☐	✓
b)	She welcomes the passengers aboard flight 157 from Hannover to London Heathrow.	☐	✓
c)	The flight will start 20 minutes later than scheduled.	✓	☐
d)	The airspace over southern Britain is not overcrowded.	☐	✓
e)	The flight will take one hour.	✓	☐
f)	They will be flying at an altitude of 25,000 feet.	☐	✓
g)	Their average speed will be 600 miles per hour.	✓	☐
h)	The weather in London is rainy.	☐	✓
i)	Temperatures will be at about 25 degrees Fahrenheit.	☐	✓

2. What describes the text you have heard the best?

✓ It is an announcement by a flight captain.
☐ It is a speech delivered by a stewardess.
☐ One of the passengers is trying to entertain the other passengers.

3. Fill in the missing information.

numbers	We will be flying with an altitude of <u>35,000 feet</u>.	Our flight will start <u>20 minutes</u> later than scheduled.
names	This is your captain speaking. My name is <u>Sandy Brown</u>.	We will land at <u>Heathrow</u> <u>Airport</u>.
towns	I'd like to welcome you aboard on flight 175 from <u>Hannover</u> to London Heathrow.	I hope you have a pleasant flight and that you enjoy your stay in <u>London</u>.

B Use of English

1. What do you need to ...?

a) send e-mails	an envelope	☐
	a computer	☑
	a TV	☐
b) listen to CDs	a radio	☐
	a stereo / CD-Player	☑
	a cassette recorder	☐
c) cool your drinks	a fridge	☑
	a stove	☐
	an electric iron	☐
d) clean the floor	a toaster	☐
	a vacuum cleaner	☑
	a microwave	☐

2. Which parts go together? Draw lines.
   a) May I open the window?
   b) I can get to school faster by bike.
   c) Could I borrow your pen, please?
   d) I'm glad I've got an apprenticeship.
   e) Would you help me with my homework, please?
   f) In my opinion the test was difficult.

3. Find the opposites.
   a) quieter
   b) fast
   c) rich
   d) empty
   e) more
   f) (to) buy

Ü-14

g) clever
  h) unsafe
  i) short
  j) never
  k) cheap
  l) (to) leave

4. **Find words with the same meaning. Choose the correct synonyms.**
   a) rock
   b) small
   c) shore
   d) Shut the door!
   e) quick
   f) job
   g) (to) call

5. **Put the verbs in the will-form. Look at Emily's plans for the week.**
   a) Next week I <u>will buy</u> a birthday present for my brother.
   b) I think I <u>will buy</u> a concert ticket for him.
   c) I hope the weather <u>will</u> be good at the weekend.
   d) Matt and I <u>will go</u> to the gym sometime next week.

6. **In English, please! Imagine the following situations and find the correct English phrase. You only have to give the English expression for the German phrase that indicates what you would say.**
   a) What did you do at/on the weekend/last weekend?
   b) I won't come/I'm not coming with you. I feel ill./I'm not feeling well./I am sick.
   c) I'm sorry, but I will be a little late.
   d) I think so, too./I agree./You're right.
   e) Let's go to the cinema.

C Reading Comprehension Test

1. **Tick (✓) the right answer to each question.**

    a) Who received an e-mail last week?
    - [ ] Paul
    - [✓] Anthony
    - [ ] Christoph

    b) How much can school fees in private schools be?
    - [✓] 15,000 pounds
    - [ ] 6 % of the family income
    - [ ] 22,000 pounds

    c) What kind of school does Anthony go to?
    - [✓] state school
    - [ ] private school
    - [ ] no school at all

    d) When does Anthony have to be at school in the morning?
    - [ ] between 9 and 9.20 a.m.
    - [ ] at 9.20 a.m.
    - [✓] at 9 a.m.

    e) Where do the children have lunch?
    - [ ] at home
    - [✓] at school
    - [ ] at a restaurant

    f) When does Anthony attend which club?
    - [✓] art on Monday, woodwork on Wednesday
    - [ ] woodwork on Friday, art on Wednesday
    - [ ] woodwork on Monday, art on Wednesday

2. **The British school system. Read the dialogue between Christopher and his English teacher. Fill in the missing parts. You don't need all of the parts given.**

   MR RYANT: "Did your friend from England answer y<u>et</u>?"

   CHRISTOPHER: "Yes he did. In his e-mail he gave me a lot of information about <u>the British school system</u>."

   MR RYANT: "That sounds good. Then you can do y<u>our presentation</u> on the British and German school system soon, can't you?"

   CHRISTOPHER: "Yes of course. I started with <u>the preparation</u> yesterday. I think I will be able to do it next Tuesday. Is that <u>alright</u> with you?"

   MR RYANT: "Of course it is. <u>I'm looking forward</u> to your presentation. What do you think about the British school system in comparison to the <u>German system</u>?"

   CHRISTOPHER: "What I most liked is that there are a lot of clubs <u>in the afternoon</u> you can join. But "assembly" sounds a bit strange to me."

   MR RYANT: "I can imagine that. <u>Have a nice day</u> Christopher and good luck with your presentation.

   CHRISTOPHER: "Thank you Mr Ryant. Bye."

3. **Answer the following questions in English.**

   a) Christoph needs the information to be able to compare the British and the German school system.

   b) It is divided into two parts: state and private school.

   c) The headmaster reads something from the bible, says a prayer and reads out general information. At the end they sing a hymn.

   d) In this subject the students learn how to choose a career and how to find a job after school.

D Text Production

1. Picture Story

A sample answer:
Sue and Tim see that their favourite band will soon be giving a concert in their home town. They go to the ticket office, but the concert is already sold out. The next morning, Tim sees an article in the newspaper in which it says that you can win tickets for the concert. He decides to take part in the competition. Sue visits a friend of hers called Ellen. Unfortunately, Ellen has broken her leg. She had bought two tickets for the concert but now that she has a broken leg she won't be able to go. Ellen gives the tickets to Sue. Sue is very happy about this and is looking forward to seeing Tim. Next day, Sue and Tim meet again. Tim has been lucky and has won the tickets in the newspaper competition. Now they both have two tickets for the concert – how funny! They decide to take two friends of theirs along. The four of them have a really nice time at the concert.

2. Letter

(address)
(date)

Europe Hotel
24 Western Street
Cambridge
CB 1 5NH
GB

Dear Sir or Madam,

We spent two nights in your hotel from August 12th to August 14th, but were very disappointed with it. Our room was dirty and the bed was broken. In addition, the food was horrible: there was a hair in my soup and the main dish was cold every day. That is the sort of standard we might have expected of a youth hostel but certainly not of a hotel.

We would be very grateful if you would return half the sum we had to pay for the weekend.

We hope to hear from you soon.

Yours faithfully,

(signature)

(your name)

> Abschlussprüfung an Hauptschulen in Bayern 2007
> Englisch

Listening Comprehension Text

Tapescript 1:
Susie is phoning her boyfriend Robert

SUSIE: Hi, Robert! It's me, Susie. What are we doing on Simon's birthday? It's this Thursday, remember?
ROBERT: Oh gosh! I totally forgot about that! What could we do? Have you got any ideas?
SUSIE: Why don't we invite him and Helen to dinner at a nice restaurant?
ROBERT: Okay. How about that new Mexican restaurant?
SUSIE: Good idea. Can you book a table for us?
ROBERT: Sure. I'll book a table for 7.30. Is that all right?
SUSIE: Fine. Can you pick me up after work?
ROBERT: No problem. See you on Thursday.

Tapescript 2:
Helen is phoning a ticket hotline

HOTLINE: Sydney Ticket Service. Can I help you?
HELEN: Yes, I'd like two tickets for the Kylie Minogue concert next Saturday, please.
HOTLINE: Okay. Would you like seats or standing room tickets?
HELEN: How much are they?
HOTLINE: The seats are 25 dollars and standing room tickets are 30 dollars.
HELEN: Why are standing room tickets more expensive?
HOTLINE: Well, you're closer to the stage and you can see Kylie much better.
HELEN: Oh, I see. Then I'd like two standing room tickets, please. Can I pay by credit card?
HOTLINE: Yes, you can pay cash or by credit card when you pick up the tickets.
HELEN: Okay, thank you very much, goodbye.

Tapescript 3:
Robert meets Simon at the concert

ROBERT: Hi, Simon. What a surprise to meet you here at a Kylie Minogue concert. Are you enjoying it?
SIMON: Yes, it's much better than I thought. She's a great singer.
ROBERT: Yeah, I think so, too.
SIMON: Helen has been a fan for many years. Now she wants to buy a Kylie Minogue T-shirt. Do you know if there's a souvenir stand here?
ROBERT: Yes, there's one round the corner. I've just bought a poster there.
SIMON: Oh, thanks, Robert. I'm sure I can get a T-shirt there, too.
ROBERT: Well, enjoy the rest of the concert. Bye.

Tapescript 4:
Helen and Simon are planning a holiday

HELEN: Hi, darling, how was work today?
SIMON: I'm so tired. I really need a holiday!
HELEN: Me, too. Guess what! When I was in town today I went to a travel agency and picked up some catalogues. Look!
SIMON: Great! So you'd like to go to Hawaii?
HELEN: Yes, I've always wanted to see Waikiki Beach.
SIMON: Yes, I know. And I'm sure you want to try surfing. But I don't want to spend all my time at the beach. I'd like to visit some of the other Hawaiian islands, too.
HELEN: Okay. Let's look at the catalogues and see what they offer.

A Listening Comprehension Test

points

Dialogue 1: Susie is phoning her boyfriend Robert
Tick (✓) the correct box. 3

a) Simon's birthday is on
   ☐ Tuesday.   ☐ Thursday.   ☐ Friday.

b) They want to have dinner at
   ☐ an Italian restaurant.   ☐ a Chinese restaurant.   ☐ a Mexican restaurant.

c) Robert is going to book a table for
   ☐ 7.30.   ☐ 7.15.   ☐ 7.00.

Dialogue 2: Helen is phoning a ticket hotline
Tick (✓) true or false. 3

	true	false
a) Helen wants four tickets for the concert.	☐	☐
b) There are tickets for 25 und 30 dollars.	☐	☐
c) Helen wants standing room tickets.	☐	☐

Dialogue 3: Robert meets Simon at the concert
Who said it? Tick (✓) the correct name. 3

	Robert	Simon
Are you enjoying it?	☐	☐
Helen has been a fan for many years.	☐	☐
I've just bought a poster there.	☐	☐

Dialogue 4: Helen and Simon are planning a holiday
Tick (✓) the correct answer. 3

a) Where did Helen go in town?
   ☐ to a travel agency
   ☐ to a ticket office

b) What famous beach does Helen want to see?
   ☐ Malibu Beach
   ☐ Waikiki Beach

c) What would Simon like to do?
   ☐ try surfing
   ☐ visit other Hawaiian islands

B Use of English

1. Tick (✓) the correct word.

a) People go there to borrow books:
☐ book shop ☐ bakery ☑ library

b) You need it to find the meaning of a word:
☐ workbook ☑ dictionary ☐ document

c) A boat that transports people and vehicles:
☑ ferry ☐ transporter ☐ fairy

d) A document you need for entering Australia:
☐ license ☑ passport ☐ student card

e) It helps you to find the right way:
☐ card ☐ ticket ☑ map

2. Which word sounds different? Cross it out.

Example: bus, run, come, ~~home~~

a) blue, too, ~~luck~~, shoe
b) cat, ~~small~~, rat, black
c) flight, ~~swim~~, kind, like
d) ~~bear~~, dear, ~~beer~~, near

3. Fill in the right word.

because – although – while – but – during

a) Nick and Susan were very tired __because__ the flight was really long.
b) __While__ Susan was waiting for their luggage, her mobile phone rang.
c) __Although__ Nick had a cold, he went swimming.
d) Susan visited Ayers Rock __but__ she didn't want to climb it.

4. Put the words in the correct order.

a) you / ever / to Australia / have / been / ?
__Have you ever been to Australia?__

b) in the sea / can / swimming / you / go / in summer / .
__You can go swimming in the sea in summer.__

c) to go / don't / in my free time / shopping / like / I / .

I don't like to go shopping in my free time.

d) two years / Joe / we / Canada / met / ago / in / .

We met Joe in Canada two years ago.

5. Fill in the correct reflexive pronoun.

Example: Could you help me with my homework? I can't do it myself.

a) "Susan, be careful with the knife, you'll hurt yourself."

b) Yesterday our guide prepared the group's barbecue, and she burnt herself very badly.

c) Our jeep wasn't repaired by a mechanic. We repaired it ourselves.

d) All the people in the group enjoyed themselves on the trip.

6. Put the sentences of the dialogue in the right order.

At the restaurant.

a) Did you enjoy the meal?

b) A glass of mineral water, please.

c) Yes, it was delicious. Can I have the bill, please?

d) Are you ready to order, madam?

e) And would you like a drink?

f) Yes, I'd like the chicken, please.

d	f	e	b	a	c

7. Which parts go together?
Fill in the numbers. One example (0) is already given.

0	Last year	1	as a cook	2	the desserts.
1	I worked	3	my job	0	a good summer job.
2	In the mornings	0	I had	3	very much.
3	I enjoyed	2	I prepared	1	from 9 am till 1 pm.

8. Read the dialogue. Fill in the missing words.

have to stay – my mother's – what about – like to go – could watch – look after – some bottles of – don't you – exciting – are having dinner – didn't you – had dinner

A: Would you _like to go_ to the cinema on Friday evening?
B: I'm sorry, but I'll _have to stay_ at home and _look after_ my little sister.
A: _What about_ your parents?
B: They _had dinner_ at a restaurant that evening.
A: Oh, what a pity! Peter says there is an _exciting_ movie at the Roxy.
B: But why _don't you_ come to my house instead? We _could watch_ some videos.
A: Great idea! I'll bring some crisps and _some bottles of_ lemonade.

Reading Comprehension Text

A train journey through Australia

0 It's a funny name for a train, but "The Ghan" is a legend in Australian history. The name is a short version of its former nickname, *The Afghan Express*. Before the first railway was built, caravans of Afghan camels carried heavy loads between Port Augusta and Alice Springs because they were able to work in the hot Australian climate. Later they also transported materials for the new railway line. Today "The Ghan" carries passengers from Adelaide to Darwin, a distance of 2,979 kilometres, in 48 hours.

1 Construction of the railway line first began in Port Augusta in 1878. Four years later it was also started in Darwin, in the north, but building a transcontinental railway line was much more difficult than most people imagined. The route had many curves, and there were often problems with floods and heavy rain that washed away bridges and tracks. It took more than 50 years until the first trains ran to Alice Springs, in 1929. Because of all the problems with this route, they later decided to build a new, straighter route, this time beginning in Adelaide. The new route was finally finished in 1957, and this time there was a plan to continue the construction through to Darwin.

2 It took another 50 years for this dream to become reality. In 1976 the route north of Alice Springs was closed, and construction didn't start again until July 2001. Two and a half years later the transcontinental railway line was finally finished. The first freight trains and passenger trains from Adelaide reached Darwin in early 2004.

3 Today "The Ghan" travels between Adelaide and Darwin two or three times a week. This trip is one of the most fascinating train journeys in the world. When you look out of the window you can enjoy the spectacular Australian landscapes. In the south you see green fields, in the center there are red deserts, and near the end of the journey in the north you travel through tropical forests. But you don't have to stay on the train for two days. Many travellers leave the train in Alice Springs to visit the famous Ayers Rock and to explore the outback for a few days, and then they continue their journey on a later train.

4 "The Ghan" offers comfortable single or double sleeper cabins. The double cabins have air conditioning and their own toilets and showers. The train also has an excellent restaurant service and a buffet car where you can buy snacks and drinks during the day. Passengers can meet in the lounge for a drink before dinner or for a game of cards. There are also video screens, which provide entertainment and information.

5 But this railway line is not only important for tourists. Freight trains as long as 1.8 kilometres carry hundreds of containers with products. Before the railway was built, huge trucks had to transport goods across the country. These 'road trains' weren't as fast or as safe as the modern trains. From its beginning to its completion, the transcontinental railway took 125 years to build, and it definitely modernized transportation in Australia.

Adapted from: www.Travelmall.com-au www.wikipedia.de

C Reading Comprehension Test

1. Find the right ending to each sentence. Tick (✓) the correct box. 6/6

a) The railway line is
- [ ] more than 3000 kilometres long.
- [✓] almost 3000 kilometres long.

b) The city of Darwin is
- [✓] in the north.
- [ ] in the outback.

c) The straighter route to the north started in
- [✓] Adelaide.
- [ ] Port Augusta.

d) "The Ghan" operates
- [ ] once a week.
- [✓] two or three times a week.

e) The double cabins have
- [✓] air conditioning.
- [ ] restaurant service.

f) In the lounge passengers can have
- [ ] a meal.
- [✓] a drink.

2. Answer the questions. You can write short answers. 5/5

a) Why did they use camels to build the first railway line?
Because they were able to work in the hot Australian climate.

b) How many days does it take to travel from Adelaide to Darwin on "The Ghan"?
2 days

c) What were three problems with the first route?
Many curves, problems with floods, heavy rain that washed away bridges and tracks.

d) What three types of landscape can you see during the journey?
Green fields, red deserts, tropical forests.

e) Where can passengers get meals on the train? (2 places)
Restaurant service and a buffet car.

E 2007-7

3. **Find a correct title (A–F) for each part (0–5) of the text.**

   There's an example at the beginning.

   A A finished project
   B A strange name
   C Travel experiences
   D A lot of problems
   E Transporting goods
   F Services on the train

0	1	2	3	4	5
B	D	A	C	F	E

4. **Which expression from the text tells you …**

   a) that "The Ghan" is very famous in Australia?

   It's a funny name for a train, but "The Ghan" is a legend in Australia history. L: 1-2

   b) that camels helped to build the railway line?

   Before the first railway was built, caravans of Afghan camels carried heavy loads... at that. L: 4-7

   c) that some passengers don't stay on the train for the whole journey?

   _____
   _____

   d) that Australian freight trains can be very long?

   _____
   _____

D Text Production

Choose either 1 (Correspondence) or 2 (Picture-based Writing).

1. Correspondence: (E-Mai) 16

Beachte: Deine E-Mail sollte mindestens 10 Sätze umfassen bzw. mindestens 80 Wörter beinhalten. Du solltest auch eigene Gedanken einbringen.
Denke an Anrede und Grußformel.

Angaben zur E-Mail:
Dieses Jahr verbringst du deine Sommerferien bei der Gastfamilie Spencer in Sydney, Australien. Du nimmst dort an einem 3-wöchigen Sprachkurs teil. Anschließend hast du noch zwei Wochen Zeit für verschiedene Aktivitäten. Du antwortest auf Mrs Spencers erste E-Mail, in der sie ihre Familie vorstellte.

Inhalt deiner E-Mail:
- Dank für die E-Mail und die schönen Familienfotos
- Information über genaue Ankunftsdaten (Datum, Uhrzeit) am Flughafen von Sydney
- Frage an Mrs Spencer nach den Transportmöglichkeiten vom Flughafen zu ihrem Haus
- Deine Pläne für den weiteren Aufenthalt nach dem Sprachkurs: Besuch von Sehenswürdigkeiten in Australien (z. B. Ayers Rock, Great Barrier Reef, Outback, Opera House und Harbour Bridge in Sydney, ...)
- Bitte um mehr Information über die interessantesten Sehenswürdigkeiten
- Wunsch, sich mit australischen Jugendlichen zu treffen
- Frage nach Möglichkeiten, den Abend zu verbringen
- Deine Begeisterung für das Surfen – Problem: Deine Angst vor Haien
- Frage nach dem Wetter im August/September und der Möglichkeit zum Surfen
- Freude auf deine Australienreise

2. Picture-based Writing: Picture Sequence (Bildfolge)   16

Schreibe einen Bericht anhand der folgenden Bilder.
Beachte: Dein Text sollte mindestens 10 Sätze umfassen bzw. mindestens 80 Wörter beinhalten.

A day in Sydney
You can start like this:
Last August the Schmitt family from Germany spent their holiday in Australia. On their first day in Sydney Mr and Mrs Schmitt, Max and Tina ...

9 am	10 am	10 am – 1 pm
Aufbruch zum Tagesausflug	Eingang zum Taronga Zoo, Sydney	Aufenthalt im Taronga Zoo, Sydney

lunchtime	afternoon	evening
Im Restaurant	Am Strand	Im Hotelzimmer

Lösungen

A Listening Comprehension Test

Dialogue 1: Susie is phoning her boyfriend Robert
Tick (✓) the correct box. (Höchstpunktzahl: 3 Punkte)

a) Simon's birthday is on
   ☐ Tuesday. ☒ Thursday. ☐ Friday.

b) They want to have dinner at
   ☐ an Italian restaurant. ☐ a Chinese restaurant. ☒ a Mexican restaurant.

c) Robert is going to book a table for
   ☒ 7.30. ☐ 7.15. ☐ 7.00.

Dialogue 2: Helen is phoning a ticket hotline
Tick (✓) true or false. (Höchstpunktezahl: 3 Punkte)

	true	false
a) Helen wants four tickets for the concert.	☐	☒
b) There are tickets for 25 und 30 dollars.	☒	☐
c) Helen wants standing room tickets.	☒	☐

Dialogue 3: Robert meets Simon at the concert
Who said it? Tick (✓) the correct name. (Höchstpunktzahl: 3 Punkte)

	Robert	Simon
Are you enjoying it?	☒	☐
Helen has been a fan for many years.	☐	☒
I've just bought a poster there.	☒	☐

Dialogue 4: Helen and Simon are planning a holiday
Tick (✓) the correct answer. (Höchstpunktzahl: 3 Punkte)

a) Where did Helen go in town?
   ☒ to a travel agency
   ☐ to a ticket office

b) What famous beach does Helen want to see?
   ☐ Malibu Beach
   ☒ Waikiki Beach

c) What would Simon like to do?
   ☐ try surfing
   ☒ visit other Hawaiian islands

B Use of English

1. Tick (✓) the correct word. (Höchstpunktzahl 2,5 Punkte)

a) People go there to borrow books:
  ☐ book shop ☐ bakery ☒ library

b) You need it to find the meaning of a word:
  ☐ workbook ☒ dictionary ☐ document

c) A boat that transports people and vehicles:
  ☒ ferry ☐ transporter ☐ fairy

d) A document you need for entering Australia:
  ☐ license ☒ passport ☐ student card

e) It helps you to find the right way:
  ☐ card ☐ ticket ☒ map

2. Which word sounds different? Cross it out. (Höchstpunktzahl: 2 Punkte)

a) blue, too, ~~luck~~, shoe

b) cat, ~~small~~, rat, black

c) flight, ~~swim~~, kind, like

d) ~~bear~~, dear, beer, near

3. Fill in the right word. (Höchstpunktzahl: 2 Punkte)

a) because

b) While

c) Although

d) but (auch: although)

4. Put the words in the correct order. (Höchstpunktzahl: 4 Punkte)

a) Have you ever been to Australia?

b) You can go swimming in the sea in summer.
   In summer you can go swimming in the sea.

c) I don't like to go shopping in my free time.
   In my free time I don't like to go shopping.

   d) Two years ago we met Joe in Canada.
   We met Joe in Canada two years ago.

5. **Fill in the correct reflexive pronoun.**

   (Jede ganz richtige Lösung wird mit einem Punkt bewertet. Für jedes falsch geschriebene Wort wird ein halber Punkt abgezogen. Höchstpunktzahl: 4 Punkte)

   a) yourself

   b) herself

   c) ourselves

   d) themselves

6. **Put the sentences of the dialogue in the right order.**

   (Nur jede vollständig richtig ausgefüllte Tabelle wird mit zwei Punkten bewertet. Ist ein Buchstabe falsch oder nicht eingetragen, wird die Aufgabe mit null Punkten bewertet. Höchstpunktzahl: 2 Punkte)

   | d | f | e | b | a | c |

7. **Which parts go together? Fill in the numbers.**

   (Andere Lösungen sind nicht möglich. Höchstpunktzahl: 3 Punkte)

0	Last year	1	as a cook	2	the desserts.
1	I worked	3	my job	0	a good summer job.
2	In the mornings	0	I had	3	very much.
3	I enjoyed	2	I prepared	1	from 9 am till 1 pm.

8. **Read the dialogue. Fill in the missing words.**

   (Sinnentstellende Abschreibfehler führen zu Punktverlust. Höchstpunktzahl: 4,5 Punkte. Pro Lücke ist ein halber Punkt vorgesehen.)

   A: Would you *like to go* to the cinema on Friday evening?
   B: I'm sorry, but I'll *have to stay* at home and *look after* my little sister.
   A: *What about* your parents?
   B: They *are having dinner* at a restaurant that evening.
   A: Oh, what a pity! Peter says there is an *exciting* movie at the Roxy.
   B: But why *don't you* come to my house instead? We *could watch* some videos.
   A: Great idea! I'll bring some crisps and *some bottles of* lemonade.

C Reading Comprehension Test

1. **Find the right ending to each sentence.
   Tick (✓) the correct box.** (Höchstpunktzahl: 6 Punkte)

   a) The railway line is
      - ☐ more than 3000 kilometres long.
      - ☒ almost 3000 kilometres long.

   b) The city of Darwin is
      - ☒ in the north.
      - ☐ in the outback.

   c) The straighter route to the north started in
      - ☒ Adelaide.
      - ☐ Port Augusta.

   d) "The Ghan" operates
      - ☐ once a week.
      - ☒ two or three times a week.

   e) The double cabins have
      - ☒ air conditioning.
      - ☐ restaurant service.

   f) In the lounge passengers can have
      - ☐ a meal.
      - ☒ a drink.

2. **Answer the questions. You can write short answers.**
   (Rechtschreibfehler führen zu Punktabzug. Höchstpunktzahl: 5 Punkte)

   a) Because they were able to work in the hot Australian climate.

   b) 2 days

   c) (It had) many curves (and there were often problems with) floods and heavy rain that washed away bridges and tracks.

   d) Green fields, red deserts, tropical forests

   e) In the restaurant, in the buffet car

3. **Find a correct title (A–F) for each part (0–5) of the text.**
   (Höchstpunktzahl: 5 Punkte)

0	1	2	3	4	5
B	D	A	C	F	E

4. **Which expression from the text tells you …**
   (Abschreibfehler führen nicht zu Punktabzug. Höchstpunktzahl: 4 Punkte)

   a) "The Ghan" is a legend in Australian history.

   b) Later they also transported materials for the new railway line.

   c) Many travellers leave the train in Alice Springs to visit the famous Ayers Rock.

   d) Freight trains as long as 1.8 kilometres carry hundreds of containers with products.

D Text Production

Choose either 1 (Correspondence: E-Mail) or 2 (Picture-based Writing).

1. **Correspondence: E-Mail**
   (Die offenere Aufgabenstellung und die in Stichpunkten formulierten Angaben ermöglichen eine größere Freiheit in der Gestaltung der E-Mail seitens der Schüler. Die angegebene Lösung ist ein Beispiel.
   16 Punkte)

   Dear Mr and Mrs Spencer, Lucy and Tim,

   Thank you very much for the email and the nice photos you sent. I will arrive at Sydney airport on Monday, August 2nd, at 7:00 am. Mrs Spencer, could you please tell me how I could go from the airport to your house?
   After the language course, I would like to travel in Australia. I would like to go to Ayers Rock and the Great Barrier Reef. Could you send me information on the most interesting places to see? I am also interested in doing some sports and I hope I can meet young Australians. What is there to do in the evenings? I am very excited about surfing but I am afraid of sharks. Are there many sharks in the ocean around Sydney? What is the weather like in August and September? Is it possible to go surfing at that time?
   I am very happy that I am travelling to Australia and I'm looking forward to meeting you! Please write again soon!

   Yours truly,
   Alexandra

2. Picture-based Writing (Bildfolge) (16 Punkte)

A day in Sydney

Last August the Schmitt family from Germany spent their holiday in Australia. On their first day in Sydney Mr and Mrs Schmitt, Max and Tina left the hotel at 9 am. They wanted to spend the day out, of course. At 10 am they arrived at the Taronga Zoo, where they bought tickets for 30 A$ each. From 10 am to 1 pm they explored the Taronga Zoo and saw many animals, like kangaroos, emus and crocodiles. Tina was happy, because she was allowed to pet a koala bear. At lunchtime they ate hot dogs and cake in a restaurant. Later, in the afternoon, they went to the beach. Although it was very windy there, Mr Schmitt took a photo of Max with a surfboard. Tina played soccer with her mother. Finally, in the evening, the Schmitt family was back in the hotel room. While Mr Schmitt and the children watched television, Mrs Schmitt wrote postcards to the family at home in Germany.

Notenschlüssel

Notenstufen	1	2	3	4	5	6
Punkte	72–64	63,5–52	51,5–38	37,5–23	22,5–12	11,5–0

Abschlussprüfung an Hauptschulen in Bayern 2008
Englisch

Listening Comprehension Text

Tapescript 1:
Mr Smith is phoning the Edinburgh Bed and Breakfast.
LANDLADY: Edinburgh Bed and Breakfast. Good afternoon, can I help you?
MR SMITH: Good afternoon. Would it be possible to make a reservation for next weekend?
LANDLADY: Let me check. Yes. What sort of room would you like?
MR SMITH: Well, there are three of us: my wife and I, and our nine-year-old daughter.
LANDLADY: I could offer you a double room with an extra bed for £75 per night, or a family room for £98 a night, including a full Scottish breakfast.
MR SMITH: Wonderful, I'll take the family room, please.
LANDLADY: Very well. May I have your name and credit card details, please?

Tapescript 2:
Mrs Smith is at a tourist office in Edinburgh.
MRS SMITH: Good morning. We're only here in Edinburgh for the weekend and we'd like to see as much of the city as possible. What would you recommend?
CLERK: Well, you might be interested in a guided walk through the historic city centre. It starts in twenty minutes if you'd like to join us.
MRS SMITH: That sounds like a good idea. What will we see on the tour?
CLARK: The tour begins with a visit to Edinburgh Castle. It's the main visitor attraction here, you know. From there, we'll see the sights in the Old Town. We'll walk along Edinburgh's oldest road. It's called "The Royal Mile" and it connects Edinburgh Castle with the Palace of Holyrood House.
MRS SMITH: What's Holyrood House?
CLERK: It's the royal palace where the Queen stays when she's in Edinburgh. But she's not here today, so we'll be able to have a guided tour of the palace. That'll be the end of our tour and you'll have seen as much as possible in your short visit to Edinburgh.
MRS SMITH: Good, we'll take three tickets.

Tapescript 3:
The Smith family is staying at the Edinburgh Bed and Breakfast.
LANDLADY: Good morning. Did you sleep well?
MR SMITH: Like a baby! It's so nice and quiet here.
LANDLADY: What would you like for your breakfast, sir? Sausages and eggs with toast?
MR SMITH: Yes, sausages, eggs and some toast for me, please. My wife might just have some toast. She'll be down in a minute.
LANDLADY: And what about your daughter? Would she like some porridge?
MR SMITH: Yes, I think so. With milk, please.
LANDLADY: And to drink? Tea or coffee?
MR SMITH: Tea for my wife and coffee for me, please. And some orange juice for our daughter.
LANDLADY: Oh, I can see they're coming now. I'll be with you in a moment.

Tapescript 4:
The Smith family wants to check in for their flight home from Edinburgh.
MR SMITH: Hello, we'd like to check in for the flight to London, please.
FLIGHT ATTENDANT: Which one would that be, sir? The one leaving at 11.05 or 12.20?
MR SMITH: The one at 11.05.
FLIGHT ATTENDANT: Ok, that's flight number 3250. May I see your tickets, please?
MR SMITH: Here you are. Do you have three seats together?
FLIGHT ATTENDANT: Let me see ... Yes, I do. It's your lucky day.
MR SMITH: Oh, great. Can I carry this bag on board with me?
FLIGHT ATTENDANT: No, I'm really sorry, sir. It's simply too large. You'll have to check it in, I'm afraid.
MR SMITH: Ok. We have two more bags to check in as well. Here they are.
FLIGHT ATTENDANT: Thanks. Here are your boarding passes. Boarding begins at 10.25. The flight departs at 11.05. First you'll need to pass through security. The security check is down the hall to your right. Have a good flight.
MR SMITH: Thank you.

A Listening Comprehension Test

points

**Dialogue 1: Mr Smith is phoning the Edinburgh Bed and Breakfast.
Underline the correct words.** 3

a) Mr Smith wants to book a room *for next week/next weekend/two weeks.*

b) He is travelling with *his wife/his two daughters/his wife and daughter.*

c) He takes a room for *£75 a night/£98 a night/£90 a night.*

**Dialogue 2: Mrs Smith is at a tourist office in Edinburgh.
Find the correct ending of each sentence.** 3

a) Edinburgh's main tourist attraction is the _____   a) Queen.

b) Palace of Holyrood House.

b) The road between the Edinburgh Castle and Holyrood House is called the ___d___   c) Old Town.

d) Royal Mile.

e) Edinburgh Castle.

c) The guided walk ends at the ___b___

**Dialogue 3: The Smith family is staying at the Edinburgh Bed and Breakfast.
True or False? Tick (✓) the correct box.** 3

	true	false
a) Mr Smith didn't sleep well.		✓
b) His wife wants sausages and eggs.		✓
c) Mr Smith wants coffee.	✓	

**Dialogue 4: The Smith family wants to check in for their flight home from Edinburgh.
Complete the sentences with the correct number *or* time.** 3

a) The number for the flight to London is ___3250___.

b) The Smith family checks in ___3___ pieces of luggage.

c) The flight to London will leave at ___11:05___.

B Use of English

1. Circle the correct word.

Example: After school Paul will *begin* – *(become)* – *begun* a carpenter.

a) I don't feel *sour* – *(safe)* – *soon*.
b) He *fell* – *(felt)* – *fly* from the tree.
c) After the meal we had a delicious *dresser* – *dressing* – *(dessert)*.
d) I'm afraid he will *(lose)* – *lie* – *lost* his money.

2. Complete the sentences using expressions from the box.

sixteen – oldest – his own age – youngest – thirteen-year-old – older

Ganesh is a genius. He is a __thirteen-year-old__ boy and also the __youngest__ person in Great Britain to have a university degree. All the university students are __older__ than he is. Ganesh enjoys playing football with other teenagers of __his own age__.

3. Write the opposites of the underlined words.

Example: The room was in complete <u>darkness</u>, but suddenly there was a bright <u>light</u>.

a) Most TV shows are <u>boring</u>, but watching a film in the cinema is __interesting__.
b) I always thought you were __clever__. But that was a <u>stupid</u> thing to say!
c) The train <u>leaves</u> Edinburgh at 10.30 a.m. – And when does it __arrive__ in London?
d) Early in the morning Tom ran to the bus stop, but he didn't __get__ the bus. He <u>missed</u> it.

4. **Match the questions with their answers.**
   Fill in the numbers. One example (0) is already given.

0	Can you tell me what time the English lesson starts?	4	Here you are
1	Can you tell me the way to the station?	3	No, you can't. I've got to visit grandma.
2	Can I help you?	1	I'm sorry, I don't know the town.
3	Can I borrow your car tonight, mum?	0	Yes, at nine-thirty.
4	Can you pass me the water, please?		You're welcome.
		2	No thanks, I'm just looking.

5. **Complete the sentences.**

   a) If the weather is fine, Tom __will play__ (play) soccer.

   b) If I __learn__ (learn) the vocabulary for the English test, I will get a good mark.

   c) Susan will go to England, if she __has__ (have) enough money.

6. **Put the sentences of the dialogue in the right order.**

   Susan's brother Tom, who __is__ (be) two years younger then she is, loves Harry Potter. Yesterday he __bought__ (buy) the last Potter book and in the evening he read over 200 pages. He __said__, (say) "I think *Harry Potter and the Deathly Hallows* is the best of the seven Potter books. I __have never read__ (never read) such a good book before!" But Susan usually __doesn't like__ (not like) reading fantasy stories. She prefers crime stories. Next week she __will go__ (go) to the bookshop to buy a new thriller.

7. **Read the dialogue. Fill in the missing words.**

were – in – ever been – would – travelling – lives – have you ever – before – who – want – ago – never been – travel – where – at – lived – drive – what

You	Scottish boy
Where do you come from?	
	I'm from Scotland. That's **in** Great Britain.
Are you **travel** [travelling] alone or with your family?	
	With my family. We're visiting my father's sister. She **lives** in Munich.
Have you [ever] been to Munich before?	
	Yes, we visited Munich two years **ago**.
Would you like to come back to Germany again some time?	
	Sure. I've **never been** to the *Oktoberfest!* I really want to see that some day.

Von 35 Punkten: 31,5

Reading Comprehension Test: A Fantasy World of Magic

1 It was Monday morning in a classroom in London. Quite a few students came into the classroom looking very tired. When the teacher asked them what was wrong, they all gave the same answer: "I spent the whole weekend reading." It may seem hard to believe that teenagers would spend a whole weekend reading. However, this time it's easy to understand, because they had been reading the newest Harry Potter book.

2 In 1997 the first Harry Potter book was published. The title in Great Britain was *Harry Potter and the Philosopher's Stone,* but in the USA it was *Harry Potter and the Sorcerer's Stone.* Both children and adults were fascinated by J K Rowling's story about a school boy who discovers that he is a wizard. The eleven-year-old Harry Potter then goes to a special boarding school for young wizards and witches.

3 That first book was followed by six more books, each one longer and more complicated than the one before. The readers were always in suspense at the end of each book, waiting for the next book to come. Consequently, fans were so eager to get the newest book that many bookstores around the world would open at midnight when a new Harry Potter book was released. Often fans wore costumes and had parties at the bookstores. The books were even specially delivered by mail to people's homes at midnight. That way, Harry Potter fans shared the experience of receiving the new books at exactly the same time.

4 What is it that makes the Harry Potter books so special? For one thing, children as well as adults enjoy reading them. The stories combine fantasy with reality. Things every reader knows and has experienced in his life – such as school experiences, enthusiasm for sports, problems with teachers – are set in a fantasy world of magic.

5 Although more than 350 million Harry Potter books have been sold, there are still people who criticize them. Some critics think that the books promote witchcraft and may be a bad influence on young people. On the other hand, J K Rowling responds that her books give a moral message. She also once stated, "I believe in God, not magic."

6 J K Rowling spent 17 years writing the seven books in her series and gave her readers all over the world something to feel good about. The books have already been translated into 65 languages, including Turkish, Vietnamese, and even Latin. Her invented words have also changed the English language. For example, the word "muggle" recently was added to the Oxford English Dictionary and defined as a clumsy person or someone who has difficulty learning a new skill.

7 Today J K Rowling is probably the richest woman in Britain. Of course, this success has changed her lifestyle. Before she started writing the Harry Potter books, she was unemployed and had to live on social welfare. Her small flat had no heating, so she went to a nearby café to write. Now she owns a big house and can afford to go on holiday and visit places all around the world whenever she wants. There will be no more Harry Potter books, but Rowling has not stopped writing. In fact, she has left the world of Hogwarts School behind her, and is now working on a fairy tale for very small children.

Adapted from: www. Spotlight-online.de (August 2007)

C Reading Comprehension Test

1. **True, false or not in the text?**
   Tick (✓) the correct answer.

	true	false	not in the text
a) One Harry Potter book has two different titles.	✓		
b) Fans were always looking forward to another Harry Potter book.	✓		
c) It took J K Rowling more than ten years to write the Harry Potter books.	✓		
d) The books are only available in Turkish, Vietnamese and Latin.		✓	
e) On her trip around the world in 2006 J K Rowling saw many interesting sights.			✓
f) J K Rowling has stopped writing books.		✓	

2. **Find a correct title (A–H) for each part (1–7) of the text.**

   One example is already given.

   A Known all over the world
   B Not everyone loves Harry Potter
   C A tired class in London
   D The second Harry Potter book
   E Potter fans
   F From poor to rich
   G The first Harry Potter book
   H The secret of the book's success

0	1	2	3	4	5	6	7
E	C	G	D	H	B	A	F

3. **Answer the questions. You can write short answers.**

   a) Why didn't the students get enough sleep on Saturday and Sunday?
   Because they're reading Harry Potter books.

b) What happened when new Harry Potter books came out?
   (give two examples)

   Often fans wore costumes and had parties at the bookstores

c) Why do some people have a problem with the Harry Potter stories?

   Because they're think that the books may be a bad influence on young people

d) How did the Harry Potter books change J K Rowling's life?
   (give 2 examples)

4. **Which expression from the text tells you …**   4

   a) … that Harry Potter finds out that he isn't just a normal boy?

   b) … that not only young people read the Harry Potter books?

   c) … that millions of people bought Harry Potter books?

   d) … that the author of the Harry Potter books did not have a job?

D Text Production

Choose either 1 (Correspondence) or 2 (Picture-based Writing). 16

1. Correspondence: (E-Mail)

Beachte: Deine E-Mail sollte mindestens 10 Sätze umfassen bzw. mindestens 80 Wörter beinhalten. Du solltest auch eigene Gedanken einbringen. Denke an Anrede und Grußformel.

Angaben zur E-Mail:
Angaben zur E-Mail: Deine ganze Familie ist von Harry Potter (Bücher und Filme) begeistert und will deshalb in diesem Jahr eine Reise durch England und Schottland machen. Ihr wollt auf den Spuren von Harry Potter wandeln. Schon letztes Jahr wolltet ihr dorthin, aber die Reise war ausgebucht. Du schreibst eine E-Mail an das Harry-Potter-Fan-Trip-Büro.

Inhalt deiner E-Mail:
- Information über dich und deine Familie
- Eure Begeisterung über Harry Potter
- Erklärung eures Reisevorhabens
- Bedauern über ausgebuchte Reise im letzten Jahr
- Bitte um Auskünfte für dieses Jahr: Angebote/verfügbare Plätze/Dauer der Reise …
- Interesse an besonderen Orten/Plätzen/Sehenswürdigkeiten (z. B. Filmschauplätze, London, Edinburgh …)
- Fragen nach Unterkunftsmöglichkeiten für Familien mit /ohne Verpflegung, Bad / Dusche …
- Bitte um Auskunft über Preise, Informationsmaterial, Stadtpläne …
- …
- Hoffnung auf baldige Antwort
- Freude auf die „Harry Potter-Reise"

2. Picture-based Writing: Picture and Prompts (Einzelbild und Impulse)

Schreibe eine Geschichte zu dem Bild. Die Stichpunkte stellen lediglich eine Anregung für den Verlauf deines Textes dar.
Beachte: Dein Text sollte mindestens 10 Sätze umfassen bzw. mindestens 80 Wörter beinhalten.

A Dream Comes True
You can start like this:
One rainy afternoon Alex Andersen (aged 21) was reading his brand-new Harry Potter book when he fell asleep. He had a wonderful dream ...

Harry Potter –
ein Wunsch – viel Geld –
Traum – Ausgeben des Geldes

Enttäuschung –
tatsächlicher Lotto-Gewinn

Lösungen

A   Listening Comprehension Test

Dialogue 1: Mr Smith is phoning the Edinburgh Bed and Breakfast.
Underline the correct words (Höchstpunktzahl: 3 Punkte)

a) Mr Smith wants to book a room *for next week/<u>next weekend</u>/two weeks*.

b) He is travelling with *his wife/his two daughters/<u>his wife and daughter</u>*.

c) He takes a room for *£ 75 a night/<u>£ 98 a night</u>/£ 90 a night*.

Dialogue 2: Mrs Smith is at a tourist office in Edinburgh.
Find the correct ending of each sentence. (Höchstpunktzahl: 3 Punkte)

a) **e** (Edinburgh Castle).
b) **d** (Royal Mile)
c) **b** (Palace of Holyrood House)

a) Queen.
b) Palace of Holyrood House.
c) Old Town.
d) Royal Mile.
e) Edinburgh Castle.

Dialogue 3: The Smith family is staying at the Edinburgh Bed and Breakfast.
True or False? Tick (✓) the correct box. (Höchstpunktzahl: 3 Punkte)

	true	false
a) Mr Smith didn't sleep well.		✗
b) His wife wants sausages and eggs.		✗
c) Mr Smith wants coffee.	✗	

Dialogue 4: The Smith family wants to check in for their flight home from Edinburgh.
Complete the sentences with the correct number *or* time.
(Höchstpunktzahl: 3 Punkte)

a) The number for the flight to London is **3250**.

b) The Smith family checks in **3** pieces of luggage.

c) The flight to London will leave at **11.05**.

B Use of English

1. Circle the correct word. (Höchstpunktzahl 2 Punkte)

a) I don't feel *sour – (safe) – soon*.

b) He *(fell) – felt – fly* from the tree.

c) After the meal we had a delicious *dresser – dressing – (dessert)*.

d) I'm afraid he will *(lose) – lie – lost* his money.

2. Complete the sentences using expressions from the box. (Höchstpunktzahl: 2 Punkte)

Ganesh is a genius. He is a **thirteen-year-old** boy and also the **youngest** person in Great Britain to have a university degree. All the university students are **older** than he is. Ganesh enjoys playing football with other teenagers of **his own age**.

3. Write the opposites of the underlined words. (Höchstpunktzahl: 4 Punkte)

a) Most TV shows are <u>boring</u>, but watching a film in the cinema is **interesting / exciting**.

b) I always thought you were **clever / smart / intelligent**. But that was a <u>stupid</u> thing to say!

c) The train <u>leaves</u> Edinburgh at 10.30 a.m. – And when does it **arrive** in London?

d) Early in the morning Tom ran to the bus stop, but he didn't **catch / get** the bus. He <u>missed</u> it.

4. Match the questions with their answers.
Fill in the numbers. One example (0) is already given. (Höchstpunktzahl: 2 Punkte)

0	Can you tell me what time the English lesson starts?	4	Here you are
1	Can you tell me the way to the station?	3	No, you can't. I've got to visit grandma.
2	Can I help you?	1	I'm sorry, I don't know the town.
3	Can I borrow your car tonight, mum?	0	Yes, at nine-thirty.

4	Can you pass me the water, please?		You're welcome.
		2	No thanks, I'm just looking.

5. **Complete the sentences.** (Höchstpunktzahl: 3 Punkte)

   a) If the weather is fine, Tom **will play** soccer.

   b) If I **learn** the vocabulary for the English test, I will get a good mark.

   c) Susan will go to England, if she **has** enough money.

6. **Put the sentences of the dialogue in the right order.** (Höchstpunktzahl: 6 Punkte)
   Susan's brother Tom, who **is** two years younger then she is, loves Harry Potter. Yesterday he **bought** the last Potter book and in the evening he read over 200 pages. He **said/says**, "I think *Harry Potter and the Deathly Hallows* is the best of the seven Potter books. I **have never read** such a good book before!" But Susan usually **doesn't like** reading fantasy stories. She prefers crime stories. Next week she **will go/is going to** the bookshop to buy a new thriller.

7. **Read the dialogue. Fill in the missing words.** (Höchstpunktzahl: 4 Punkte)

You	Scottish boy
Where do you come from?	
	I'm from Scotland. That's **in** Great Britain.
Are you **travelling** alone or with your family?	
	With my family. We're visiting my father's sister. She **lives** in Munich.
Have you ever been to Munich before?	
	Yes, we visited Munich two years **ago**.
Would you like to come back to Germany again some time?	
	Sure. I've **never been** to the *Oktoberfest!* I really want to see that some day.

C Reading Comprehension Test

Vokabelhinweise: sorcerer (am. Engl.) (Z. 14): Zauberer; suspense (Z. 23): Spannung; enthusiasm (Z. 38): Begeisterung; to promote sth. (Z. 43 f.): etw. fördern; social welfare (Z. 62): Sozialhilfe

1. **True, false or not in the text?**
   Tick (✓) the correct answer. (Höchstpunktzahl: 3 Punkte)

		true	false	not in the text
a)	One Harry Potter book has two different titles.	✗	☐	☐
b)	Fans were always looking forward to another Harry Potter book.	✗	☐	☐
c)	It took J K Rowling more than ten years to write the Harry Potter books.	✗	☐	☐
d)	The books are only available in Turkish, Vietnamese and Latin.	☐	✗	☐
e)	On her trip around the world in 2006 J K Rowling saw many interesting sights.	☐	☐	✗
f)	J K Rowling has stopped writing books.	☐	✗	☐

2. **Find a correct title (A–H) for each part (1–7) of the text.**
   (Höchstpunktzahl: 6 Punkte)

0	1	2	3	4	5	6	7
E	C	G	E	H	B	A	F

3. **Answer the questions. You can write short answers.**
   (Rechtschreibfehler führen zu Punktabzug.) (Höchstpunktzahl: 6 Punkte)

   a) Why didn't the students get enough sleep on Saturday and Sunday?

   They didn't sleep because they spent the whole weekend reading (Harry Potter).

   b) What happened when new Harry Potter books came out?
   (give two examples)

   Many bookstores around the world would open at midnight.

   Often fans wore costumes and had parties at the bookstores.

   The books were even specially delivered by mail to people's homes at midnight.

c) Why do some people have a problem with the Harry Potter stories?

Some critics think that the books promote witchcraft

The books may be a bad influence on young people.

d) How did the Harry Potter books change J K Rowling's life? (give 2 examples)

Today J K Rowling is probably the richest woman in Britain.

J K Rowling was unemployed and had to live on social welfare.

Now she owns a big house and she can afford to go on holiday.

4. **Which expression from the text tells you ...** (Höchstpunktzahl: 4 Punkte)

(Abschreibfehler führen nicht zu Punktabzug.)

a) ... that Harry Potter finds out that he isn't just a normal boy?

A school boy who discovers that he is a wizard.

b) ... that not only young people read the Harry Potter books?

Children as well as adults enjoy reading them./Both children and adults were fascinated by J K Rowling' story.

c) ... that millions of people bought Harry Potter books?

More than 350 million Harry Potter books have been sold.

d) ... that the author of the Harry Potter books did not have a job?

She was unemployed./She had to live on social welfare.

D Text Production

(Wähle zwischen der E-Mail und der Bildergeschichte. Setze das zweisprachige Wörterbuch gezielt ein.)

1. **Correspondence: E-Mail** (Höchstpunktzahl: 16 Punkte)

(Hier sollst du unter Beweis stellen, dass du frei formulieren kannst. Achte jedoch darauf, alle angegeben Punkte zum Inhalt in deine Mail einzubauen. Die angegebene Lösung ist ein Beispiel.)

Dear Sir or Madam,

My name is ... I am ... years old and I live with my parents and my little sister in ... My family and I really love the Harry Potter books. We have read all of them and seen the films as well. That is why we would love to see the Harry Potter locations in England and Scotland this summer.

When we wanted to do the trip last year your tour was sold out. We were so disappointed. Now, I would like to ask you for some information about tours this year. Is it still possible to book a tour? How many days do the tours take?

We would really like to see the Harry Potter film locations in Scotland and Oxford. Are London or Edinburgh also included in the trip? Is there special accomodation that you offer for families? We would like to have accommodation that includes meals and has rooms with a shower or a bath.

Could you also send us some price lists, city maps and brochures for information? Thank you very much in advance. I'm looking forward to your answer. My family and I can't wait to start our "Harry Potter tour".

Yours faithfully,

2. **Picture-based Writing: Picture and Prompts (Einzelbild und Impulse)**

   A Dream Comes True

   One rainy afternoon Alex Andersen (aged 21) was reading his brand-new Harry Potter book when he fell asleep. He had a wonderful dream …

   Alex dreamed that Harry Potter came flying into his room. "That's Harry Potter! I can't believe it!", Alex cried out. "Yes, it's me.", Harry said. "You have one wish. Tell me what you like to have." Alex didn't think long about that. "I would like to have so much money that I can buy everything." So Harry took his wand, said some magic spells and suddenly thousands of bank notes came out of his wand.

   Alex couldn't believe his eyes. He was happy because now he could buy whatever he liked. He could get one of the best seats to watch a football match, for example. He could also drive in a racing car like Michael Schumacher, or see his favourite band as often as he liked. Suddenly, he woke up and realized that this was only a dream.

   Alex was a bit disappointed but then his mother came in with a letter from the national lottery. Now he really couldn't believe his eyes. He was the winner of last week's lottery! So his dream has finally come true.

Notenschlüssel

Notenstufen	1	2	3	4	5	6
Punkte	70–61.5	61,0–50,5	50,0–37,5	37,0–22,5	22,0–11,5	11,0–0

Listening Comprehension Text

Tapescript 1:
Sam is talking to his boss Mrs Smith.
SAM: You wanted to see me?
MRS SMITH: Yes, ... You know, Sam. During your three weeks' work experience at our hospital, you really did a great job. And you also have good grades in school. But there is a problem.
SAM: What is it?
MRS SMITH: Well, Sam, some patients have complained about your tattoo.
SAM: But it's only a little dragon on my hand!
MRS SMITH: Actually, it's quite a large dragon. It gives our patients the wrong impression of you.
SAM: Really?
MRS SMITH: Yes, many patients really don't like your tattoo. It makes them feel uncomfortable and they are a bit afraid of you.
SAM: Do you mean I have no chance of getting a job here? I really hoped I could work here after I finished school.
MRS SMITH: I'm sorry, Sam, but with this tattoo, we simply can't give you a job.

Tapescript 2:
After work Sam meets his friend Megan.
MEGAN: What's wrong, Sam?
SAM: Well, you know how excited I was about my work experience at the hospital. It's a really great place to work.
MEGAN: Yes, you told me. Maybe they will offer you a job after you finish school.
SAM: No, they don't want me. It's because of my tattoo.
MEGAN: What! Well, you can get it removed.
SAM: But that's difficult.
MEGAN: Oh, no, I heard it's very easy. You can just use a cream to remove tattoos.
SAM: But this tattoo is permanent. When I got it my parents had to give their permission. And at first my mom did not want to sign the piece of paper.
MEGAN: Let's look on the internet and see if we can find some tattoo removal cream for you.
SAM: Maybe I should call my doctor first. What do you think?

Tapescript 3: Sam talks to his doctor.
DOCTOR: So, young man. What can I do for you?
SAM: Well, ah, ... I have a tattoo and I don't want it anymore. My friend told me about a cream that removes tattoos. Can you tell me if it works?
DOCTOR: A cream is not a good idea. I wouldn't use it.
SAM: What should I do then?
DOCTOR: Well, the easiest thing to do is to cover it with your clothing. Wear long sleeves.
SAM: No, I would have to wear gloves to cover it. Look here, it's on my hand.
DOCTOR: Oh, it's going to be a problem. Tattoos are very difficult to remove. Laser treatment is best but that is expensive and it can take up to a year for the tattoo to disappear.
SAM: Will it go away completely?
DOCTOR: Sometimes. But I'm sorry to say that you might always have some colour left in your skin. It has green, red or yellow in it, doesn't it?
SAM: Yes. the dragon is green, the eyes are red and the tail is yellow.
DOCTOR: Well, unfortunately, red, green and yellow inks tend to leave a mark that will not go away.
SAM: Oh, dear, that doesn't sound good.
DOCTOR: Look, why don't you speak to your parents and see what they think.
SAM: Ok, I'll do that. Thank you.

Tapescript 4: Sam is talking to his mother on the way to the doctor.
MOM: Oh Sam, I never wanted you to get that tattoo! This is going to be painful and expensive. I'll pay the $200 for your first treatment but you're going to pay for the rest.
SAM: But Mom, I'll need at least five more treatments! That'll cost $1,000!
MOM: Don't complain! You wanted that tattoo! I just hope you learn your lesson.
SAM: I've heard it hurts, Mom. I'm a little bit scared.
MOM: Don't worry, you'll be fine. By the way, I'm glad that the job at the hospital is more important to you than your tattoo.

A Listening Comprehension Test   points

Dialogue 1: Sam is talking to his boss Mrs Smith.
Listen and mark the correct endings.   2

1. Sam has worked at
   ☐ a nursing home
   ☐ a hospital
   ☐ a kindergarten

2. At school Sam has good
   ☐ friends
   ☐ grades
   ☐ classes

3. Some patients have complained about his
   ☐ work
   ☐ clothes
   ☐ tattoo

4. Many patients are
   ☐ angry
   ☐ afraid
   ☐ happy

Dialogue 2: After work Sam meets his friend, Megan.
Listen and fill in the missing word in each sentence.   4

1. It's really a ___great___ place to work.
2. Maybe they will offer you a _____ after you finish school.
3. And my _____ didn't want to sign that piece of paper.
4. Maybe I should call my _____ first.

Dialogue 3: Sam talks to his doctor.
True or False? Mark the correct box.   4

		true	false
1.	Sam's friend told him about a cream that removes tattoos.	☐	☐
2.	The doctor says that the cream is no problem.	☐	☐
3.	Sam could cover the tattoo with his cap.	☐	☐
4.	Laser treatment can take one year.	☐	☐
5.	The tattoo will always go away completely.	☐	☐
6.	Sam has a red dragon.	☐	☐
7.	Red, green and yellow inks tend to leave a permanent mark.	☐	☐
8.	The doctor says Sam should talk to his parents.	☐	☐

**Dialogue 4: Sam is talking to his mother on the way to the doctor.
There's one mistake in each sentence. Cross out the wrong word.** 2

1. I will pay the $300 for your treatment today.
2. But Mom, I will need at least four more laser treatments.
3. I'm a little bit sad.
4. I'm happy that the job at the hospital is more important to you than your tattoo.

B Use of English

1. Cross out the word which doesn't fit. 1,5

    a) application   interview   CV   ~~bill~~

    b) cellphone   ~~handy~~   mobile   telephone

    c) ~~map~~   menu   order   starter

2. In this letter there are 7 mistakes. Find them and cross them out. 3,5

Hi Mike,
~~Mai~~ name is Robert. I'm twelve ~~jears~~ old and I live in ~~bavaria~~. I've got a brother. He's older ~~then~~ me. He likes sports, but I ~~prifer~~ computer games. Next week ~~i~~ will get an MP3-player. That's ~~graet~~! ~~Waht~~ about you? Please write soon.
Yours,
Robert

3. Complete the sentences using prepositions. 3

Usually we meet <u>at</u> my uncle's house __on__ Sundays. 5 o'clock __at in__ the afternoon we always have a cup __of__ coffee. Uncle Sam's dog sleeps __under__ the table. We go home __after__ dinner.

4. Write the words of the sentences in the correct order. 3

    a) already / got / have / new / tattoo / you / your / ?
    b) week / last / I / an / appointment / had /.
    c) from / it / protect / the sun / !

5. **Put in the right form of the verbs.**

Birgit went (go) to Australia in 2005. She left (leave) Germany with her parents. Two months ago, Birgit started (start) a new job at the supermarket. She really enjoys (enjoy) working there. Her parents don't like (not like) the house they live in. So they will move (move) into a big farmhouse next month.

6. **Read the dialogue and fill in the missing words. Look at the answers first.**

Robert: *Where* did you learn English?
Birgit: At a school in London.
Robert: When did you arrive in Australia?
Birgit: I arrived in 2005.
Robert: Who came with you?
Birgit: My parents.
Robert: How did you travel?
Birgit: I travelled by plane.
Robert: Why did you choose Australia?
Birgit: I chose Australia, because I love the warm climate.
Robert: Where do your parents originally come from?
Birgit: They come from Europe.
Robert: What are your plans for the future?
Birgit: I'd like to buy a farm in the outback.

7. Tom and Susan are talking on the phone. Match the parts of the dialogue. You don't need one of Susan's statements.

	Tom
1	What about meeting at the youth club at 7 pm tonight?
2	Oh! What about tomorrow night?
3	Oh, I'm sorry to hear that!
4	Tell me, what happened?
5	Oh, my goodness! Okay …, so see you tomorrow morning at the bus stop.

	Susan
a)	No way. This week I'm not allowed to go out at night. My mother is angry with me.
b)	Never mind. It's already Thursday.
c)	OK. I'll be there in half an hour.
d)	Sorry, I can't. My Mom is going to drive me to school.
e)	Sorry, but I can't come.
f)	Well, I didn't take the dog for a walk yesterday. So we had a bad surprise in the living room.

1	2	3	4	5
e	a	b	f	d

Reading Comprehension Test: Body Art

A Are you a fan of body art? Have you ever thought of getting pierced or tattooed? Among young people in the United States tattoos and piercings are becoming more and more popular. Some people admire this and even call it "body art". Other people don't understand why anyone would want such "ugly things" on their bodies.

B Why do so many young Americans like body art? People's motivations for piercing or tattooing could be anything from attracting a romantic partner to just trying to be different from others. A tattoo can be a reminder of an important event in someone's life or it can show their taste in fashion. It can also make people appear "cool" to their social group and so increase their status. Jonathan Daulton, aged 19, has ten piercings on his face. "Honestly, I do it to shock people", says the University of Nebraska student. Another student, 21-year-old Marina Harding from Seattle, Washington, gives her reason as: "This is how I express myself." She likes to wear a T-shirt that says: "I dress this way to shock you!" This statement refers to her bright green hair, and piercings on her tongue, lip, nose and eyebrow, as well as six earrings in each ear. Marina also has eight tattoos and she wants to get more. She says, "I love body art."

C On the other hand, doctors point out that certain health risks go along with these forms of self-expression. Possible health problems caused by piercings could be infections and sometimes a long healing time, even up to 12 months. In addition, the American Dental Association has given a serious warning about tongue piercings. The metal in the tongue hits the teeth during eating and speaking. This can cause cracks or broken teeth. The piercing even sometimes damages nerves in the tongue so that some people can no longer speak or swallow properly. Problems with tattoos can include allergic reactions to the ink and also infections. For both piercings and tattoos, the most serious risks are actually life-threatening. If a tattoo parlor doesn't take basic health precautions such as using new latex gloves and new needles for each customer, Hepatitis B and AIDS infections are a big risk.

D Although you may be happy with your tattoos and piercings while you're still young, what about when you get older? If, for example, you have your boyfriend's or girlfriend's name tattooed on your arm and the relationship falls apart, what would you do about the tattoo? Tattoos are painful and expensive to remove. That is why many people prefer temporary tattoos. These last for a few days or even a week. You can remove them easily with oil or lotion. So you can enjoy the fun of "body art" with a new design whenever you like, without any risk.

Reproduced by permission of Oxford University Press. Adapted from Read and Reflect 2: Academic Reading Strategies and Cultural Awareness by Lori Howard with Jayme Adelson-Goldstein
© Oxford University Press 2004.

C Reading Comprehension Test

1. Match the title (1–5) to the correct part of the text (A–D).
There is one extra title. 4

1. Permanent or temporary
2. Serious warnings
3. A popular trend
4. Reasons for body art
5. History of tattoos

A	B	C	D

2. Answer the questions. You can write short answers. 8

a) What is body art? Give two examples.

b) What is the text on Marina Harding's T-shirt?

c) What are health problems caused by tattoos or piercings? Name **four**.

d) What basic health precautions should a tattoo parlor take? (**Two** examples)

e) Why do many people prefer temporary tattoos? (**Two** reasons)

3. True, false or not in the text? Mark the correct answer. 3

	true	false	not in the text
a) Some people get a tattoo to attract a new partner.	☐	☐	☐
b) Tattoos are not allowed at school.	☐	☐	☐
c) Jonathan has got 10 piercings all over his body.	☐	☐	☐
d) Most doctors say that tattoos and piercings are no problem.	☐	☐	☐
e) Health problems caused by body art are not paid by health insurance.	☐	☐	☐
f) A piercing through the tongue can damage nerves.	☐	☐	☐

4. **Which lines from the text tell you ...** 3

    lines

    a) ... that some people get a tattoo to remember something special in their lives? _____
    b) ... that piercings can take up to a year to heal? _____
    c) ... that removing tattoos hurts and costs a lot of money? _____

D Text Production

Choose either 1. (Correspondence) or 2. (Picture-based Writing). 16

1. Correspondence: E-Mail

Beachte: Deine E-Mail sollte mindestens 10 Sätze umfassen bzw. mindestens 80 Wörter beinhalten. Du kannst auch eigene Gedanken einbringen.
Denke an Anrede und Grußformel.

Angaben zur E-Mail: Du hast im letzten Sommer Chris aus Liverpool kennengelernt. Seitdem seid ihr in E-Mail-Kontakt. Ihr habt euch vorgenommen, in diesen Sommerferien eine Woche gemeinsam zu verbringen. Folgende E-Mail hast du soeben von Chris erhalten. Antworte darauf.

> Hi,
> Have you finished your exams? I hope so.
> I'm just planning our holiday. Let's go to London from 12 to 20 August. What do you think? You'll find some information in the attachment.
> CU,
> Chris
> P.S. I just got a tattoo! It's awesome!!!

Inhalt deiner E-Mail:
– Informiere über deine laufenden Prüfungen.
– Du freust dich auf das geplante Treffen in den Ferien.
– Stimme Chris' Vorschlag zu. Oder:
  Mache einen eigenen Vorschlag, z. B. Reise ans Meer oder an einen See.
– Begründe deine Entscheidung, z. B. Freizeitaktivitäten und gemeinsame Unternehmungen im Urlaub.
– Reagiere auf das Tattoo:
  • mindestens 2 Fragen dazu
  • deine Meinung
  • bitte um ein Foto.
– Du hoffst auf baldige Antwort.

2. Picture-based Writing: Picture story

Schreibe eine Geschichte zu den Bildern.
Beachte: Dein Text sollte mindestens 10 Sätze umfassen bzw. mindestens 80 Wörter beinhalten.

Two for one
You can start like this:
One Saturday morning Ian Carpenter was taking his dog Rocky for a walk. On his way to the park, he passed a hairdresser's shop. There was a poster in the shop window ...

Lösungen

A   Listening Comprehension Test

(Die Dialoge werden von einer CD abgespielt. Beantworte die zugehörigen Aufgaben. Rechtschreibfehler werden in diesem Prüfungsteil nicht bewertet.)

**Dialogue 1: Sam is talking to his boss Mrs Smith.
Listen and mark the correct endings.** (Höchstpunktzahl: 2 Punkte)

1. ☐ a nursing home
   ☒ a hospital
   ☐ a kindergarten

2. ☐ friends
   ☒ grades
   ☐ classes

3. ☐ work
   ☐ clothes
   ☒ tattoo

4. ☐ angry
   ☒ afraid
   ☐ happy

**Dialogue 2: After work Sam meets his friend, Megan.
Listen and fill in the missing word in each sentence.** (Höchstpunktzahl: 4 Punkte)

1. It's really a **great** place to work.
2. Maybe they will offer you a **job** after you finish school.
3. And my **mom** didn't want to sign that piece of paper.
4. Maybe I should call my **doctor** first.

**Dialogue 3: Sam talks to his doctor.
True or False? Mark the correct box.** (Höchstpunktzahl: 4 Punkte)

	true	false
1. Sam's friend told him about a cream that removes tattoos.	☒	☐
2. The doctor says that the cream is no problem.	☐	☒
3. Sam could cover the tattoo with his cap.	☐	☒
4. Laser treatment can take one year.	☒	☐
5. The tattoo will always go away completely.	☐	☒
6. Sam has a red dragon.	☐	☒

7. Red, green and yellow inks tend to leave ☒ ☐
   a permanent mark.

8. The doctor says Sam should talk to his ☒ ☐
   parents.

**Dialogue 4: Sam is talking to his mother on the way to the doctor.
There's one mistake in each sentence. Cross out the wrong word.**

(Höchstpunktzahl: 2 Punkte)

1. I will pay the ~~$ 300~~ for your treatment today.

2. But Mom, I will need at least ~~four~~ more laser treatments.

3. I'm a little bit ~~sad~~.

4. I'm ~~happy~~ that the job at the hospital is more important to you than your tattoo.

B   Use of English

(In diesem Prüfungsteil darfst du kein Wörterbuch verwenden. Solltest du Rechtschreibfehler machen, die das Wort so verändern, dass man den Inhalt oder den Sinn nicht mehr versteht, verlierst du Punkte.)

1. Cross out the word which doesn't fit.   (Höchstpunktzahl 1,5 Punkte)

a) bill

Vokabeln zum Wortfeld „Bewerbung": application – Bewerbung; CV – Lebenslauf;
interview – Vorstellungsgespräch

b) handy

Vokabeln zum Wortfeld „Telefon": cellphone / mobile – Mobiltelefon, Handy;
„handy" wird im englischen Sprachgebrauch nicht verwendet!

c) map

Vokabeln zum Wortfeld „Restaurant": menu – Speisekarte; order – Bestellung; starter – Vorspeise

2. In this letter there are 7 mistakes. Find them and cross them out.

(Höchstpunktzahl: 3,5 Punkte)

Hi Mike,

~~Mai~~ name is Robert. I'm twelve <u>jears</u> old and I live in <u>bavaria</u>. I've got a brother. He's older <u>then</u> me. He likes sports, but I <u>prifer</u> computer games. Next week <u>i</u> will get an MP3-player.
That's <u>graet</u>! <u>Waht</u> about you? Please write soon.

Yours,
Robert

3. **Complete the sentences using prepositions.** (Höchstpunktzahl: 3 Punkte)

Usually we meet <u>at</u> my uncle's house **on** Sundays. **At/Around/Before** 5 o'clock **in** the afternoon we always have a cup **of** coffee. Uncle Sam's dog sleeps **under/beside/beneath/next to/near** the table. We go home **after/for/before** dinner.

4. **Write the words of the sentences in the correct order.** (Höchstpunktzahl: 3 Punkte)

   a) Have you already got your new tattoo?/Have you got your new tattoo already?

   b) Last week I had an appointment./I had an appointment last week.

   c) Protect it from the sun!

5. **Put in the right form of the verbs.** (Höchstpunktzahl: 6 Punkte)

Birgit **went** (go) to Australia in 2005. She **left** (leave) Germany with her parents. Two months ago, Birgit **started** (start) a new job at the supermarket. She really **enjoys** (enjoy) working there. Her parents **don't like** (not like) the house they live in. So they **will move/are moving/are going to move** (move) into a big farmhouse next month.

6. **Read the dialogue and fill in the missing words. Look at the answers first.** (Höchstpunktzahl: 3 Punkte)

Robert: **Where** did you learn English?
Birgit: At a school in London.
Robert: **When** did you arrive in Australia?
Birgit: I arrived in 2005.
Robert: **Who** came with you?
Birgit: My parents.
Robert: **How** did you travel?
Birgit: I travelled by plane.
Robert: **Why** did you choose Australia?
Birgit: I chose Australia, because I love the warm climate.
Robert: **Where** do your parents originally come from?
Birgit: They come from Europe.
Robert: **What** are your plans for the future?
Birgit: I'd like to buy a farm in the outback.

7. **Tom and Susan are talking on the phone. Match the parts of the dialogue. You don't need one of Susan's statements.**

(Höchstpunktzahl: 4 Punkte)

1	2	3	4	5
e	a	b	f	d

C Reading Comprehension Test

(In diesem Prüfungsteil darfst du ein zweisprachiges Wörterbuch benutzen.)

Vokabelhinweise: to admire (Z. 6): bewundern; reminder (Z. 15): eine Erinnerung an; taste (Z. 17): Geschmack; to increase (Z. 19): steigern; to express (Z. 26): ausdrücken; to refer to (Z. 29): sich beziehen auf; to point out (Z. 35): darauf hinweisen, deutlich machen; in addition to (Z. 41): zusätzlich; to swallow (Z. 49): schlucken; to include (Z. 50): beinhalten; life-threatening (Z. 53): lebensgefährlich; health precautions (Z. 55): Gesundheitsvorkehrungen; relationship (Z. 64): Beziehung; temporary (Z. 68): vorübergehend, zeitlich begrenzt; to remove (Z. 70): entfernen

1. **Match the title (1–5) to the correct part of the text (A–D). There is one extra title.**

(Höchstpunktzahl: 4 Punkte)

A	B	C	D
3	4	2	1

2. **Answer the questions. You can write short answers.**

(Höchstpunktzahl: 8 Punkte)

a) Piercings and tattoos

b) I dress this way to shock you.

c) Infections, Aids, Hepatitis B, cracks or broken teeth, damage to nerves, allergic reactions, long healing time

d) Using new latex gloves and new needles for each customer.

e) They only last for a few days or even a week. You can remove them easily. You can enjoy the fun of "body art" with a new design whenever you like, without any risk.

3. True, false or not in the text? Mark the correct answer.

(Höchstpunktzahl: 3 Punkte)

		true	false	not in the text
a)	Some people get a tattoo to attract a new partner.	☒	☐	☐
b)	Tattoos are not allowed at school.	☐	☐	☒
c)	Jonathan has got 10 piercings all over his body.	☐	☒	☐
d)	Most doctors say that tattoos and piercings are no problem.	☐	☒	☐
e)	Health problems caused by body art are not paid by health insurance.	☐	☐	☒
f)	A piercing through the tongue can damage nerves.	☒	☐	☐

4. Which lines from the text tell you …

(Höchstpunktzahl: 3 Punkte)

		lines
a)	… that some people get a tattoo to remember something special in their lives?	15–16
b)	… that piercings can take up to a year to heal?	39–41
c)	… that removing tattoos hurts and costs a lot of money?	66–67

D Text Production

(Auch in diesem Prüfungsteil darfst du ein zweisprachiges Wörterbuch verwenden. Entscheide dich bei der Bearbeitung <u>entweder</u> für die Email <u>oder</u> für die Bildergeschichte.)

1. Correspondence: E-Mail (Höchstpunktzahl: 16 Punkte)

(In der Aufgabenstellung findest du Hinweise zum Inhalt der E-mail. Baue möglichst viele dieser Inhalte in deinen Text ein. Wenn du willst, kannst du diese Vorgaben auch teilweise durch eigene Ideen ergänzen oder ersetzen. Wichtig ist, dass der Umfang der E-mail mindestens 10 Sätze beträgt. Achte beim Schreiben der E-mail auch darauf, dass du den Empfänger begrüßt und dich am Ende von ihm verabschiedest.)

Hello Chris,

Thanks for your mail. I haven't finished my exams yet. My last exam is one week before I come to see you in Liverpool. I'm very happy that we'll meet during the holidays.

It's a great idea to go to London together! We can visit some interesting places and maybe we can go to a concert in the city. I'm also looking forward to seeing Buckingham Palace.

It's cool that you got a tattoo. Did it hurt? I am curious to see what it shows. Could you send me a photo?

Please write back soon!

Bye,
Michael

2. Picture-based Writing: Picture and Prompts (Einzelbild und Impulse)

(Höchstpunktzahl: 16 Punkte)

(Bevor du mit dem Schreiben beginnst, solltest du die Abbildungen genau betrachten. Finde den Höhepunkt der Geschichte heraus (Ians bester Freund ist sein Hund Rocky) und überlege dir weitere Punkte, die für das Verständnis der Bildergeschichte wichtig sind (Angebot im Schaufenster des Friseurs, Rockys neuer Haarschnitt, Ians Reaktion auf das Aussehen seines Hundes). Verfasse anschließend einen Text, der die gesamte Bildergeschichte erzählt. Denke daran, auch die wörtliche Rede zu verwenden.)

One Saturday morning Ian Carpenter was taking his dog Rocky for a walk. On his way to the park, he passed a hairdresser's shop. There was a poster in the shop window. It said: *Get a new hairstyle. Your best friend is free!* Both Ian and his dog Rocky had very long hair.

So they went inside the shop and Ian told Julian and Lucy, the hairdressers, that he wanted to take the offer[1]. "But where's your best friend?" the hairdressers asked. "He's right there!" Ian answered and pointed to his dog Rocky.

"Please cut the dog's hair," Julian told Lucy. Lucy was not happy about this job. She took Rocky to a part of the room that was hidden[2] behind a curtain. While Julian was styling Ian, Lucy was busy with Rocky.

When Julian had finished, Ian checked himself in the mirror. He liked his new hairstyle and paid Julian for it. "What about Rocky?" Ian asked. Lucy opened the curtain and brought Rocky. The dog had almost no hair left and looked like he was styled for the circus. Ian was really shocked about the dog's new look!

1 offer – Angebot
2 to hide – verbergen

Notenschlüssel

Notenstufen	1	2	3	4	5	6
Punkte	70–61	60,5–50	49,5–36	35,5–22	21,5–11	10,5–0

Notenschlüssel für Legastheniker

Notenstufen	1	2	3	4	5	6
Punkte	66,5–59,5	59–48,5	48–34,5	34–21,5	21–10	9,5–0

Listening Comprehension Text

Tapescript 1:
FATHER: What's the matter, Mary? Is everything OK? You don't look very happy.
MARY: Oh, Dad, I don't know what to do.
FATHER: What do you mean?
MARY: This morning as I was walking past some of my friends outside school, they all started laughing. I felt like they were laughing at me.
FATHER: What did you do then?
MARY: Oh, I just walked away.
FATHER: Mmm.
MARY: And the other thing is ... well, I've been getting some really horrible emails recently. I can't see who they're from because I don't recognise the addresses.
FATHER: Oh, no.
MARY: But whoever the people are, they're saying horrible things about me. You know, things that aren't true at all.
FATHER: Think for a moment. I mean, maybe you've said something to somebody at school and made them angry.
MARY: Well, I did have an argument with Susan last week.
FATHER: OK.
MARY: And I know she's still angry with me, because she hasn't spoken to me since then.
FATHER: But would Susan send you horrible emails?
MARY: No, no ...well ... I don't think so.
FATHER: OK. Look. When you tell me you are receiving horrible emails, it sounds to me – well –, as if it could be cyber bullying or something like that. I think we should phone the police.
MARY: The police?
FATHER: Yes, they have a special helpline for information about cyber bullying. They can tell us what to do.

Tapescript 2:
POLICE: Hello. What can I do for you?
MARY: Well, um ... I've got a big problem. I don't think I can solve it on my own.
POLICE: OK. Can you tell me what it is?
MARY: Yes, people are sending me nasty emails.
POLICE: Oh ...
MARY: And lies about my private life are being posted on the internet.
POLICE: I see. And how are things at school at the moment?
MARY: Well, nobody in my class talks to me. They all ignore me.
POLICE: I see ... Have you had an argument with anybody recently?
MARY: Yeah. Last week I had a big fight with my best friend.
POLICE: And what's your friend's name?
MARY: Susan. But she's not my friend anymore.
POLICE: Susan. And she's in your class, you said.
MARY: Yes.
POLICE: Right. Now, the first thing you should do is to speak to your parents about what's going on.
MARY: Yes. In fact it was my Dad's idea that I contact you.
POLICE: Good. Next point: do not open any emails from people you don't know.
MARY: Oh, OK. I never thought of that.
POLICE: And the last thing ...
MARY: Yes?
POLICE: Save all the nasty messages you get.
MARY: Save them? Why?
POLICE: Well, any nasty messages you receive will help us to find out who's behind this problem.
MARY: I understand. OK. Great. Thanks for your help.

Tapescript 3:
POLICE: Hello Susan.
SUSAN: Hello.
POLICE: Please come in and have a seat.
SUSAN: Thank you.
POLICE: Now, do you know why I wanted to talk to you today?
SUSAN: No, not really.
POLICE: It's about your friend, Mary.
SUSAN: Mary?
POLICE: Yes. Mary told us you two were best friends and she trusted you.
SUSAN: Yes.
POLICE: And she also told us that she gave you the password for her email account. Is that true?
SUSAN: Um ... yes, it is.

POLICE: And is it true that you used Mary's account to send nasty emails to Mary's friends?
SUSAN: Er ...
POLICE: And that Mary's friends thought Mary had sent those emails?
SUSAN: But it was only a joke! Honestly! Mary and I had an argument and I was ... I was really angry with her!

POLICE: But using Mary's email account isn't a joke! It's a serious matter, Susan. Do you know what it's called?
SUSAN: No.
POLICE: Cyber bullying.

A Listening Comprehension Test

points

Dialogue 1: Mary (15) has just come home from school and is talking with her father.
Listen and tick (✓) a, b, or c.

5

1. What happened to Mary outside school? People ...
   a) ☐ ... laughed at her.
   b) ☐ ... talked behind her back.
   c) ☐ ... pointed at her.

2. What did Mary do then? She ...
   a) ☐ ... stopped.
   b) ☐ ... got angry.
   c) ☐ ... walked away.

3. When did Mary have an argument with Susan?
   a) ☐ Last month
   b) ☐ Last week
   c) ☐ Last Tuesday

4. Why does her father want to contact the police?
   To get information about ...
   a) ☐ ... Susan.
   b) ☐ ... other students.
   c) ☐ ... what to do.

5. Who is Mary having a problem with?
   a) ☐ The police
   b) ☐ Friends
   c) ☐ Teachers

Dialogue 2: After talking with her father, Mary calls a police helpline. True or False? Mark the correct box.   3

	true	false
1. Mary can solve the problem on her own.	☐	☐
2. Lies about Mary can be found on the Internet.	☐	☐
3. Susan and Mary are still friends.	☐	☐
4. The police officer tells Mary to talk to her parents.	☐	☐
5. The police officer tells Mary to read all incoming mails.	☐	☐
6. Mary should keep the nasty messages.	☐	☐

Dialogue 3: Susan is at a police station. A police officer will ask her some questions. There's one mistake in each sentence. Cross out the wrong word and write down the correct one.   3

1. Mary told us that you two were good friends. _____
2. Susan sent nice emails to Mary's friends. _____
3. Using Mary's internet account isn't a joke. _____

B Use of English

1. Find the opposite of the underlined word.   4

Example: My jeans are too <u>short</u>. My sister's jeans are too <u>long</u>.

a) You enter the cinema through the <u>entrance</u> and you leave it through the ___exit___.

b) Peter can't ___spend___ all his money. He wants to buy a new MP3-player, so he must <u>save</u> at least € 5 a month.

c) I <u>go to bed</u> at 8 p.m. when I have to ___get up___ early next morning.

d) Spending your holiday at home is usually very <u>cheap</u>, but going to another country can be quite ___expensive___.

2. **Fill in the correct word.**

   Example: colour/coloured/colourful
   Your pullover is a nice <u>colour</u>. I like <u>colourful</u> things.

   a) want to/will/would
      I am sure that we <u>will</u> visit New York next year, because we all <u>want to</u> see the Statue of Liberty.

   b) interest/interested in/interesting.
      The new movie is really <u>interesting</u>. Everybody is <u>interested in</u> it.

3. **Which word sounds different? Cross it out.**

   Example: could – ~~shout~~ – should – would – wood

   a) fight – site – night – ~~wait~~ – light
   b) run – come – son – sun – ~~long~~
   c) shoe – true – ~~cute~~ – through – two
   d) key – keep – meat – ~~friend~~ – treat

4. **Fill in the correct word. Use each word only once.**

   ~~attractive~~ – best – carefully – ~~happy~~ – ~~terribly~~ – well – worse

   a) Jane is an <u>attractive</u> girl, but she sings <u>terribly</u>.
   b) Mike is one of the <u>best</u> players on his football team.
   c) When all the students work <u>carefully</u>, the teacher is really <u>happy</u>.
      <u>well</u>

5. **Fill in the correct pronoun.**

   Example: This is Peter. <u>He</u> is 15 years old.

   Peter is 15 years old. <u>His</u> older brother is 17 years old. <u>They</u> live together with <u>their</u> parents in a nice little house. <u>Their</u> mother is a nurse. <u>She</u> works in a hospital. Peter's father works for an international company. <u>He</u> really loves his job and always says, "I love <u>my</u> job because <u>I</u> can meet people from all over the world."

6. **Complete the sentences.** 3

   Example: If the weather is fine, we will go (go) swimming.
   a) If we go to South Africa we will visit (visit) a national park.
   b) If my father lends (lend) me his camera, I will be able to take really good photos.
   c) I'll be (be) very happy, if we can go to my friend's birthday party.

7. **Fill in the right form of the verbs.** 3

   John (play) has played computer games with his friends for years. They usually (meet) meet at a club. It's the same club where John (work) works every weekend. Yesterday some of the club members (find) found bad messages on the net. At the moment, they (talk) re talking to a police officer. The police officer (come) 'll come to their school next week.

8. **Finish the dialogue.** 5

   You are staying in Sydney and want to go to Canberra.

   At the station

Ticket assistant	You
Good afternoon! How can I help you?	Good afternoon. I want to go to Canberra.
Single or return?	Single, please. How much is the ticket?
That will be $ 48. Here's your ticket.	Thank you. When will we arrive in Canberra?
It arrives at 10 o'clock.	Where does the train leave?
From platform 7.	Thanks very much.
You're welcome. Have a nice trip.	

Reading Comprehension Test: Getting the Message

Throughout history, people have searched for ways to communicate across great distances. In early Egypt, messages were sent by runners, and later by messengers on horseback. In 90 BC, the Chinese government started the first postal service. However, real progress in communication technology only began in the 18th century, when developments like the typewriter, new signal systems and photography became the basis for later progress. Above all, the key to new communication technology was the first use of electricity in the 1800s.

In the 1840s Samuel Morse, an American inventor, created the first successful telegraph machine and used electricity to send messages in Morse code. The new telegraph technology also led to Scottish inventor Alexander Bain's invention of the first fax machine in 1843. On 10 March 1876, Alexander Graham Bell spoke into an experimental telephone, saying, "Mr. Watson, come here. I want to see you." His assistant in the next room heard and understood this first telephone message. Soon after that, the Danish inventor Valdemar Poulsen developed the world's first telephone answering machine. That happened in 1898. Then – within less than fifty years, between 1902 and 1951 – modern communication began. Radio, motion pictures, television, tape recorders and even computers had all been invented and were on their way to popular success.

At first, digital electronic messages were only possible between computers belonging to the same network. The first real breakthrough to email as we know it today happened in 1971, when Ray Tomlinson successfully sent an email message from one computer network to another. He used the symbol for the English word "at" to identify the different networks. That symbol is the @, which you always see in email addresses. Asked what he wrote, Tomlinson said he didn't remember exactly. "It was something like *QWERTYUIOP.*" In the early 1990s, the internet increased email use. Now email is a very fast and inexpensive way to send messages worldwide.

In the late 1990s, people began sending a new kind of electronic message. They used their mobile phones to send text messages. Neil Papworth, an engineer, sent the first personal text message to a friend in Great Britain on 3 December 1992. The message was "Merry Christmas" (abbreviated: *Merry Xmas*).

One might say that teenagers have had the greatest influence on the development of texting. They were the first group to use mobiles more for texting than for actually talking on the phone. They have even created a special language for texting, sometimes called "textese" or "txtese". As with Papworth's first message, one single letter or number can replace a syllable. Thus, "See you later" becomes "CU L8R". There has been some discussion among teachers and parents about whether textese will cause the "end of the English language". However, most teenagers could never imagine texting without it

adapted from: Paul A. Davies, Information technology: 1000 headwords (Oxford Bookworms Library Factfiles, Stage 3). Oxford University Press, Oxford 2007.

C Reading Comprehension Test

1. Tick the correct box.

a) The first postal service was started by …

☐ … messengers on horseback.
☐ … runners.
☑ … the Chinese government.
☐ … the Egyptian government.

b) Modern communication began in the 20th century within less than …
- [ ] … 25 years.
- [ ] … 40 years.
- [x] … 50 years.
- [ ] … 80 years.

c) Why didn't emailing become popular before 1971? Because …
- [ ] … no one had a password.
- [x] … it was only possible between computers of the same network.
- [ ] … people preferred to send text messages on their mobiles.
- [ ] … computers had not been invented yet.

d) In 1971 there was a real breakthrough in communication technology. It was the first …
- [ ] … telephone call.
- [ ] … telegram.
- [ ] … text message.
- [x] … use of @ in emails.

2. Read the text. Then put the following facts into the right order.

a) Teachers and parents discussed textese.
b) Samuel Morse invented a code for telegraph messages.
c) People sent text messages on their mobile phones.
d) People sent emails using the internet.
e) The typewriter, signal systems, and photography were invented.
f) Ray Tomlinson sent a message that started with "Q".
g) A Scottish inventor created the first fax machine.

1	e
2	b
3	g
4	f
5	d
6	c
7	a

3. Read the text. Answer the questions. Write **short** answers.

a) How were messages sent in early Egypt?
By runners later by messengers on horseback

b) Who did Mr Bell call on his experimental telephone?
Mr. Watson and his assistant

c) What was invented soon after the telephone?
telephone answering machine

d) Who was the engineer who sent the first personal text message by mobile phone?

   Nill Pe

e) Who were the first group to use mobiles more for texting than for speaking?

   teenagers

f) What is the "textese" form for *later*?

   _L8R_

D Text Production (Dictionaries are allowed.)

Choose either 1. (Correspondence) or 2. (Picture-based Writing). 16

1. Correspondence: E-Mail

Beachte: Deine E-Mail sollte mindestens 10 Sätze umfassen bzw. mindestens 80 Wörter beinhalten. Du kannst auch eigene Gedanken einbringen. Denke an Anrede und Grußformel. Angaben zur E-Mail: Du willst Erfahrungen im Ausland sammeln. Deshalb bist Du auf der Suche nach einem Ferienjob. Im Internet findest du folgende Anzeige:

*hier: Kinderanimateur/Betreuer

Schreibe eine Bewerbung. Achte auf folgende Inhaltspunkte:
- Gib an, wo du die Anzeige gefunden hast.
- Stelle dich kurz vor.
- Erkläre, warum du dich für diesen Job interessierst.
- Begründe, warum du für den Job geeignet bist.
- Gehe ausführlich auf deine sportlichen Fähigkeiten ein.
- Erkundige dich nach Verdienst und Unterkunftsmöglichkeiten.
- Weise auf den Lebenslauf mit Foto im Anhang hin.

2. Picture-based Writing: Picture story   16

Schreibe eine Geschichte zu den Bildern.
Beachte: Dein Text sollte mindestens 10 Sätze umfassen bzw. mindestens 80 Wörter beinhalten.

A frightening experience at a wildlife park
You can start like this:
Last September the Huber family planned a trip to South Africa ...

- Information suchen
- Reise buchen

- Weihnachtsferien 2009
- geführte Tagestour
- wilde Tiere

- Reifenpanne
- ein Löwe nähert sich

- Flucht in Fahrerkabine
- Ängste des Jungen

Lösungen

A Listening Comprehension Test

(Die folgenden Dialoge hörst du immer je zweimal. Höre genau auf die Anweisungen und versuche, die Aufgaben zu lösen. Sieh dir den Text erst an, wenn du nicht mehr weiterkommst.)

Dialogue 1: Mary (15) has just come home from school and is talking with her father.
Listen and tick (✓) a, b, or c. (Höchstpunktzahl: 5 Punkte)

1. a) [X] laughed at her
2. c) [X] walked away
3. b) [X] Last week
4. c) [X] what to do
5. b) [X] Friends

Dialogue 2: After talking with her father, Mary calls a police helpline.
True or False? Mark the correct box. (Höchstpunktzahl: 3 Punkte)

		true	false
1.	Mary can solve the problem on her own.		[X]
2.	Lies about Mary can be found on the Internet.	[X]	
3.	Susan and Mary are still friends.		[X]
4.	The police officer tells Mary to talk to her parents.	[X]	
5.	The police officer tells Mary to read all incoming mails.		[X]
6.	Mary should keep the nasty messages.	[X]	

Dialogue 3: Susan is at a police station. A police officer will ask her some questions. There's one mistake in each sentence. Cross out the wrong word and write down the correct one. (Höchstpunktzahl: 3 Punkte)

1. ~~good~~: best
2. ~~nice~~: nasty
3. ~~internet~~: email

B Use of English

(Anhand der folgenden Aufgaben werden dein Wortschatz, deine Grammatik-Kenntnisse und deine Ausdrucksfähigkeit in kommunikativen Situationen beurteilt. In diesem Prüfungsteil darfst du <u>kein</u> Wörterbuch benutzen.)

1. Find the opposite of the underlined word. (Höchstpunktzahl 4 Punkte)

(Hier musst du die gegenteilige Bedeutung des unterstrichenen Wortes auf Englisch einsetzen. Es kann dir helfen, wenn du das unterstrichene Wort ins Deutsche übersetzt. Achte auch auf den Satzzusammenhang.)

a) You enter the cinema through the <u>entrance</u> and you leave it through the <u>exit</u>.

(entrance: *Eingang; Ausgang:* exit)

b) Peter can't <u>spend</u> all his money. He wants to buy a new MP3-player, so he must <u>save</u> at least € 5 a month.

(to spend: *(Geld) ausgeben; sparen:* to save)

c) I <u>go to bed</u> at 8 p.m. when I have to <u>get up</u> early next morning.

(to go to bed: *Schlafen gehen; aufstehen:* to get up)

d) Spending your holiday at home is usually very <u>cheap</u>, but going to another country can be quite <u>expensive</u>.

(cheap: *preiswert; teuer:* expensive)

2. Fill in the correct word. (Höchstpunktzahl 2 Punkte)

a) I am sure that we <u>will</u> visit New York next year, because we all <u>want to</u> see the Statue of Liberty.

(Das Signalwort „next year" weist auf die Verwendung der Zukunftsform „will" hin. In der nächsten Lücke macht nur „want to" (wollen) Sinn. „Would" (würde) ergibt im Satzzusammenhang keinen Sinn.)

b) The new movie is really <u>interesting</u>. Everybody is <u>interested in</u> it.

(interesting: *interessant;* to be interested in sth.: *sich für etw. interessieren;* interest: *das Interesse*)

3. Which word sounds different? Cross it out. (Höchstpunktzahl: 2 Punkte)

(Spreche dir, wenn du zu Hause übst, die einzelnen Wörter laut vor, dann fallen dir die Unterschiede in der Aussprache leichter auf.)

a) wait   b) long   c) cute   d) friend

4. Fill in the correct word. Use each word only once. (Höchstpunktzahl: 3 Punkte)

(Hier geht es darum, dass du erkennst, ob du ein Adjektiv oder ein Adverb einsetzen musst.)

a) Jane is an <u>attractive</u> girl, but she sings <u>terribly</u>.

(attractive *(Adjektiv);* terri**bly**: *furchtbar* – Die Endung -ly zeigt, dass es sich um ein Adverb handelt: *Auf welche Art und Weise singt Jane?:* terribly)

b) Mike is one of the <u>best</u> players on his football team.
   (one of the best: *einer der besten*)

c) When all the students work <u>carefully</u>/<u>well</u> the teacher is really <u>happy</u>.
   (*Adverbien:* carefully: *gewissenhaft;* well: *gut; Adjektiv:* happy: *glücklich/zufrieden – Wie ist der Lehrer/die Lehrerin?:* happy)

5. Fill in the correct pronoun. (Höchstpunktzahl: 5 Punkte)

(Hier musst du jeweils das richtige persönliche Fürwort *(I, you, he/she/it, we, you, they)* oder besitzanzeigende Fürwort *(my, your, his/her/its, our, your, their)* eintragen. Achte auf die vorangehenden Sätze, dann kannst du aus dem Sinn erschließen, welches Fürwort du einsetzen musst. Auch gibt dir das Verb einen Hinweis: eine Form mit der Endung -s bedeutet, dass du als persönliches Fürwort nur *he, she* oder *it* verwenden kannst, z. B. in "<u>She</u> work<u>s</u> *in a hospital"*.)

Peter is 15 years old. <u>His</u> older brother is 17 years old. <u>They</u> live together with <u>their</u> parents in a nice little house. <u>Their</u> mother is a nurse. <u>She</u> works in a hospital. Peter's father works for an international company. <u>He</u> really loves his job and always says, "I love <u>my</u> job because <u>I</u> can meet people from all over the world."

6 Complete the sentences. (Höchstpunktzahl: 3 Punkte)

(Hier geht es darum, If-Sätze vom Typ I zu vervollständigen. Dabei musst du darauf achten, dass im Hauptsatz *will* + die Grundform des Verbs und im Nebensatz *if* + die *simple present*-Form des Verbs steht.)

a) If we go to South Africa we <u>will</u> visit a national park.

b) If my father <u>lends</u> me his camera, I will be able to take really good photos.

c) I <u>will be</u> very happy, if we can go to my friend's birthday party.

7 Fill in the right form of the verbs. (Höchstpunktzahl: 3 Punkte)

(Hier sollst du die richtige Zeitform des Verbs einsetzen. In Klammern ist jeweils der Name der Zeitform angegeben, sodass du sie in der Kurzgrammatik schnell findest. Achte auch auf die Signalwörter. Sie sind in der Lösung fett markiert.)

John <u>has played</u> *(present perfect)*/<u>has been</u> <u>playing</u> *(present perfect progressive)* computer games with his friends **for years**. They **usually** <u>meet</u> *(simple present)* at a club. It's the same club where John <u>works</u> *(simple present)* **every weekend**. **Yesterday** some of the club members <u>found</u> *(simple past)* bad messages on the net. **At the moment**, they <u>are</u> <u>talking</u> *(present progressive)* to a police officer. The police officer <u>will</u> <u>come</u> *(will-future)*/<u>is</u> <u>going</u> <u>to come</u> *(going to-future)* to their school **next week**.

8 Finish the dialogue. (Höchstpunktzahl: 5 Punkte)

(Hier musst du einen Dialog vervollständigen, wie er im Alltag vorkommen kann. Du kannst wählen, ob du ein *single ticket* (Ticket nur für die Hinfahrt), oder ein *return ticket* (Ticket für die Hin- und Rückfahrt) kaufen möchtest.)

TICKET ASSISTANT: Good afternoon! How can I help you?
YOU: Good afternoon. I'd like to go / I'd like a ticket to Canberra.
TICKET ASSISTANT: Single or return?
YOU: Single / Return please. How much is the ticket?
TICKET ASSISTANT: That will be $ 48. Here's your ticket.
YOU: Thank you. When does (will) the train arrive in Canberra?
TICKET ASSISTANT: It arrives at 10 o'clock.
YOU: Where does / From which platform does the train leave?
TICKET ASSISTANT: From platform 7.
YOU: Thanks very much.
TICKET ASSISTANT: You're welcome. Have a nice trip.

C Reading Comprehension Test

(In diesem Prüfungsteil darfst du ein zweisprachiges Wörterbuch benutzen.)

Vokabelhinweise: *message* (Z. 3): Botschaft; *BC (before Christ)* (Z. 4): vor Christus; *progress* (Z. 6): Fortschritt; *development* (Z. 7 f.): Entwicklung; *inventor* (Z. 16): Erfinder; *soon after* (Z. 22): kurz darauf; *to increase* (Z. 41): zunehmen, erhöhen; *influence* (Z. 52): Einfluss; *development* (Z. 52): Entwicklung

1. Tick the correct box. (Höchstpunktzahl 4 Punkte)

   a) ... the Chinese government.

   b) ... 50 years.

   c) ... it was only possible between computers of the same network.

   d) ... use of @ in emails.

2. Read the text. Then put the following facts into the right order.

(Höchstpunktzahl 5 Punkte)

(Lies für diese Aufgabe den Text noch einmal ganz durch, um danach die angegebenen Fakten in die richtige Reihenfolge zu bringen.)

a) Teachers and parents discussed textese.

b) Samuel Morse invented a code for telegraph messages.

c) People sent text messages on their mobile phones.

d) People sent emails using the internet.

1	e
2	b
3	g
4	f

e) The typewriter, signal systems, and photography were invented.

f) Ray Tomlinson sent a message that started with "Q".

g) A Scottish inventor created the first fax machine.

5	d
6	c
7	a

3. **Read the text. Answer the questions. Write <u>short</u> answers.**

(Höchstpunktzahl 6 Punkte)

(Lies den Text noch einmal und beantworte die Fragen in Stichpunkten.)

a) by runners and later by messengers on horseback

b) Mr Watson / his assistant

c) the (telephone) answering machine

d) Neil Papworth

e) teenagers

f) L8R

D Text Production

(Auch in diesem Prüfungsteil darfst du ein zweisprachiges Wörterbuch verwenden. Entscheide dich bei der Bearbeitung <u>entweder</u> für die Email <u>oder</u> für die Bildergeschichte.)

1. **Correspondence: E-Mail**   (Höchstpunktzahl: 16 Punkte)

(In der Aufgabenstellung findest du Vorgaben zum Inhalt der E-mail. Baue möglichst alle Vorgaben in deinen Text ein. Du kannst auch eigene Ideen hinzufügen. Wichtig ist, dass der Umfang der E-mail mindestens 10 Sätze (mindestens 80 Wörter) beträgt und in sich schlüssig ist. Beachte, dass es sich hier um eine Bewerbung handelt und du somit nicht in der Umgangssprache schreiben kannst. Achte beim Schreiben der E-mail auch darauf, dass du den Empfänger begrüßt und dich am Ende von ihm verabschiedest.
Der Empfänger ist in diesem Fall eine Frau. Da du nicht weißt, ob Frau Byrd verheiratet ist *(Mrs)* oder nicht *(Miss)*, musst du die neutrale Anrede *(Ms)* benutzen.)

Vokabelhinweise:
hours – hier: Geschäftszeiten, Arbeitszeiten
location – Ort
duration – Dauer
temporary – zeitlich begrenzt
description – Beschreibung
skills required – erforderliche Fähigkeiten
how to apply – „wie man sich bewirbt" = Bewerbungsverfahren
employer – Arbeitgeber

E 2010-15

Dear Ms Byrd,

I found your summer job offer on the ROBIN HOOD CLUBS web page.

My name is Daniel Wagner, and I am a 15-year-old student from Bamberg, Germany. I am interested in helping the child minder at Robin Hood Clubs in Kyllini, because I would like to have a summer job that makes it possible for me to work with children and practise my English. I am also a great fan of Greece, where I have already been on holiday with my parents.

I am used to looking after children because I have two younger sisters, aged 7 and 5. I often take care of them in the afternoons because both my parents work.

I like sports very much. I am a member of my school's swimming team, and I often play badminton with my friends. The languages I speak are German and English.

Could you please send me some information about how much I would earn and about where I would stay while working at Robin Hood Clubs?

I have attached my photo and CV to this mail, and I am looking forward to hearing from you.

Yours sincerely,
Daniel Wagner

2. **Picture-based Writing: Picture story** (Höchstpunktzahl: 16 Punkte)

(Bevor du mit dem Schreiben beginnst, solltest du die Abbildungen genau betrachten. Berücksichtige beim Schreiben die inhaltlichen Vorgaben.)

Last September the Huber family planned a trip to South Africa. They found a lot of information about Kruger National Park on the internet and they booked their holiday, including a trip to the park.

During the Christmas holiday 2009, the Hubers started their guided day trip to Kruger National Park. They were all very excited and hoped that they would see some wild animals.

Soon after they had gone into the park, their tour truck had a flat tyre. When the tour guide, who was also the driver, was changing the wheel, little Annika Huber saw a lion coming towards them and started to scream. Everybody quickly fled into the driver's cabin of the truck. Now the lion was right in front of the truck and waited. Annika's brother Tim was very scared and thought they would all die. But after some minutes, the lion just went away. The Hubers were very happy because the lion wasn't hungry that day!

Notenschlüssel

Notenstufen	1	2	3	4	5	6
Punkte	68–60	59,5–49	48,5–37	36,5–22	21,5–12	11,5–0

Listening Comprehension Text

Part 1:
JENNY: Hello. Um. ... Heathrow Airport, please.
TAXI DRIVER: Heathrow? OK. Where are you flying to?
JENNY: Sorry?
TAXI DRIVER: Which terminal is it?
JENNY: It's terminal ... um ... wait a second ... one, I think. To Munich.
TAXI DRIVER: OK. Which airline did you say?
JENNY: British Airways. At 11.30.
TAXI DRIVER: British Airways? Ah, that's terminal 5.
JENNY: Really?
TAXI DRIVER: Yeah, all British Airways flights go from there.
JENNY: Let me check. Um. Yeah, yeah. You're right. *(Taxi hält an.)*
TAXI DRIVER: OK. Here we are. That's £23.50, please.
JENNY: Thank you.
TAXI DRIVER: Oh, thanks. Do you need any help with your bags?
JENNY: That'd be lovely. They're quite heavy.
TAXI DRIVER: OK. You grab a trolley and I'll get everything out of the boot.
JENNY: Thanks.
TAXI DRIVER: There you are. When did you say your flight was?
JENNY: 11.30.
TAXI DRIVER: Oh, you'd better hurry then. It's quarter to eleven already.
JENNY: Really? 10.45. Oh no!

Part 2:
JENNY: Hello.
Man from BA: Hello there.
JENNY: I'm booked on the 11.30 flight to Munich but I haven't been able to check in yet.
MAN FROM BA: That's OK. Can I have your passport, please? Thanks. How many items of luggage are you checking in? Two?
JENNY: No, just this big suitcase.
MAN FROM BA: OK. And that bag? Is that your hand luggage?
JENNY: That's right. I'm not too late, am I?
MAN FROM BA: No, no. Can you put the suitcase on the scales, please?
JENNY: It's quite heavy, but I hope it's not ... too heavy.
MAN FROM BA: Hmm ... seventeen kilos. That's fine. The weight limit is 23.
JENNY: Oh, good. Do you think I could have a window seat?
MAN FROM BA: Let me have a look. Um. No, I'm afraid that's not going to work. And there are no aisle seats left either.
JENNY: Oh, OK.
MAN FROM BA: Sorry about that. So, that's 16 B.
JENNY: 16 B. OK. Thanks.
MAN FROM BA: Boarding begins at five past eleven so you've got 10 minutes.
JENNY: Great. Thanks.
MAN FROM BA: Gate 15.
JENNY: OK. Is that far to walk?
MAN FROM BA: No, no, it's very close. You can see it from here.

Part 3:
VOICE: Good morning, ladies and gentlemen. This is an important announcement for passengers checked in on flight BA 942 to Munich. This flight is scheduled to leave at 11.30. Because of a problem we are having with the onboard computer system there will be a short delay. We apologise for this situation. You will understand that our engineers are doing everything they can to make sure the flight leaves as soon as possible. We would ask all passengers to stay near the gate and wait for further announcements. We hope to give you an update in the next ten to fifteen minutes. Once again, we apologise for the delay.

Part 4:
YOUNG WOMAN: Hey, are you also waiting for the flight to Munich?
JENNY: Yeah.
YOUNG WOMAN: Have you been on holiday here?
JENNY: No, no. I was doing a language course, in Brighton.
YOUNG WOMAN: Oh, Brighton! I know Brighton well. And did you enjoy it?
JENNY: Yeah, it was excellent. And I was staying with a family there. They were great, too.

YOUNG WOMAN: Oh, so it was quite intensive then. One week, did you say?
JENNY: No, two weeks. And yesterday I was in London, in Brixton ...
YOUNG WOMAN: Brixton. OK.
JENNY: ... visiting some friends and doing some shopping.
YOUNG WOMAN: Lovely.
JENNY: And last night we all went to a musical ...
YOUNG WOMAN: OK.
JENNY: And then in the evening when we got back I forgot to set my alarm clock ...
YOUNG WOMAN: Oh dear.
JENNY: ... and this morning I missed the train.
YOUNG WOMAN: Oh no.
JENNY: So I had no time for breakfast and had to get a taxi instead.
YOUNG WOMAN: Well, you made it.
JENNY: Yeah. The taxi was expensive, but the driver was really friendly.
(Pause)
YOUNG WOMAN: Look, would you like a cup of coffee?
JENNY: That's a good idea. I need to eat something as well.
YOUNG WOMAN: Shall we go over there to that café?
(Jingle)
JENNY: Wait a second. That could be for us.
YOUNG WOMAN: Oh no. Not another delay!
VOICE: Thank you for being so patient, ladies and gentlemen. BA 942 to Munich is now ready for boarding. Please have your passport *(fade out)* and boarding card ready when you come forward to the gate. Thank you again. We wish you a pleasant flight.

A   Listening Comprehension Test   points

Part 1: Jenny is in a taxi on her way to the airport. While listening fill in the missing numbers.   4

1. Jenny's plane leaves at _____.

2. Jenny's plane goes from terminal _____.

3. Jenny's journey to the airport costs £ _____.

4. Jenny arrives at the airport at _____.

Part 2: Jenny is checking in at the British Airways desk. While listening tick (✓) the correct ending.   3

1. Jenny has got ...
   a) ☐ ... a bag and a suitcase.
   b) ☐ ... a bag and two suitcases.
   c) ☐ ... two bags and a suitcase.

2. Jenny's suitcase weighs ...
   a) ☐ ... 17 kilos.
   b) ☐ ... 20 kilos.
   c) ☐ ... 23 kilos.

3. Jenny gets …
   a) ☐ … an aisle seat.
   b) ☐ … a middle seat.
   c) ☐ … a window seat.

Part 3: At the gate Jenny hears an announcement. There's one mistake in each sentence. While listening cross out the wrong word. 4

1. This is an important announcement for passengers booked in on flight BA 942 to Munich.
2. Because of a problem that we are having with the onboard computer system there will be a small delay.
3. You will understand that our pilots are doing everything they can to make sure the flight leaves as soon as possible.
4. We would ask all passengers to sit near the gate and wait for further announcements.

Part 4: At the gate a young woman talks to Jenny. Are the sentences true (T) or false (F)? While listening tick (✓) the correct box. 4

	T	F
1. Jenny has been on holiday in England.	☐	☐
2. In Brighton Jenny stayed with friends.	☐	☐
3. Jenny has been in England for two weeks now.	☐	☐
4. In London Jenny visited a music school.	☐	☐
5. In the evening Jenny set her alarm clock.	☐	☐
6. Jenny didn't have any breakfast.	☐	☐
7. Jenny's taxi driver was very nice.	☐	☐
8. Jenny hasn't got time to go to the airport café.	☐	☐

B Use of English

1. Computers
Complete the text. Use four different words from the box. There is an example at the beginning (0).

> make – ~~need~~ – put – ~~save~~ – ~~send~~ – surf – ~~turn on~~ – ~~write~~

Every day I (0) **turn on** my computer. Sometimes I (1) _need_ it for my homework because we often have to (2) _write_ texts. Once I lost an important text so now I always (3) _save_ everything immediately. There are also a lot of photos on my computer. I (4) _send_ the nicest ones to my friends.

2. At a restaurant
Write the word that matches the definition. There is an example at the beginning (0).

Example: This person serves food in a restaurant.   w a i t e r

a) A list of all the food served in a restaurant.   m e n u
b) It shows how much you have to pay for your meal.   b i l l
c) The part of a restaurant where the meals are prepared.   k i t c h e n
d) You use this for cutting your food.   k n i f e

3. Sounds
Find the word from the box which sounds the same. Write it on the line. There is an example at the beginning (0).

> bread – ~~date~~ – made – now – paid – pair – pie – stone – were – won

Example: eight – **date**

a) there   _pair_
b) own   _stone_
c) said   ~~made~~ _bread_
d) why   _pie_

4. In London

Fill in the words in their right form. There is an example at the beginning (0).

London is the (**0** big) **biggest** city in England. The London Underground is the (**1** old) _oldest_ underground system in the world. People use it because it is (**2** fast) _faster_ than the buses. Taking a taxi is (**3** expensive) _more expensive_ than using public transport. One of the (**4** good) _best_ ways to get around the centre of London is on foot.

5. A day out

Tell the story in the <u>simple past</u>. Use six different words from the box. There is an example at the beginning (0).

> not buy – do – go – have – ~~meet~~ – spend – not visit – watch

Yesterday Susan (**0**) **met** her friend Beth in town. First the girls (**1**) _went_ to a café and (**2**) _had_ a milkshake. Then they (**3**) _did_ some shopping. They (**4**) _spent_ an hour in a clothes shop but they (**5**) _didn't buy_ anything. Later they (**6**) _watched_ an interesting film at the cinema.

6. Different situations

What would you say? Tick (✓) the correct box. There is an example at the beginning (0).

Example: Can I call you back later?
☐ I hope so.   ☐ It's not time.   ✓ Sure.

a) Let's have a drink.
☐ Me too.   ✓ Good idea.   ☐ I'm afraid so.

b) Thanks a lot for your help.
☐ Please.   ☐ I agree.   ✓ You're welcome.

c) How are you?
✓ Fine, thanks.   ☐ Great, that's nice.   ☐ Sorry, it's bad.

Reading Comprehension Test: Helping people connect?

He could be any young American guy. He dresses in jeans and T-shirts. He lives with his girlfriend. He's into computers and the internet. But this 27-year-old is different from other people his age. He started a company that millions of people all over the world use. A movie has been made about him. TIME, a US news magazine, made him Person of the Year 2010.

His name? Mark Zuckerberg, founder of Facebook, self-made billionaire, and the man who wants to make the world "a more open place by helping people connect and share". Mark grew up near New York City. As a boy he was interested in computer programming. Once he even created a network for the family home, calling it ZuckNet. Mark went to Harvard, a famous university in Massachusetts, to study Psychology and Computer Science. In 2003 he started Facebook as a way for students at his university to communicate with each other. But Facebook didn't stay at Harvard.

Today, around 700 million people have Facebook accounts. It's easy to set up a profile and, what's more, it's free. You can start posting information about yourself immediately: your likes and dislikes, your school or employment history, photographs, videos, and anything else that you want to share. You can also change your privacy settings. Information can be seen by your friends, by friends of your friends or by anybody.

Facebook, like other social networks, has many advantages. You can contact individuals and groups easily. You can exchange information and make arrangements. You can tell your friends where you've been and show them the photos you've taken. You can direct people to the music, DVDs or websites you're enjoying.

Using Facebook doesn't cost anything, but hundreds of Facebook employees still have to be paid. How does that work? Through advertising, of course. When you join Facebook, you soon see advertisements which match your age, your education and your interests. Although you can decide how much of your profile other people see, you can't decide if Facebook passes on your data to other companies. You didn't know that? Maybe it's time to inform yourself.

There are other problems with social networks. Many young people post information about themselves and upload personal photographs. Of course there are some users who aren't worried about protecting their data. They don't mind if everyone can see them and read about them. Imagine these people apply for a job. Would they be happy if their future boss could see what they do in their free time and who their friends are?

Users say Facebook helps them to communicate with friends. That's true, of course, but what sort of "communication" is it? And what sort of "friends" do they have in the virtual world of Facebook? Maybe we can communicate with our friends just as well, if not better, on the telephone or in face-to-face conversations. And what could be a more personal way of communicating with someone than sending them a handwritten letter?

C Reading Comprehension Test

1. **Find the correct title (A–H) for each part of the text. Use each letter only once. One title is already matched. There is one extra title.** 6

    A Sharing your life with the world

    B Who pays? You?

    C Positive aspects

    D A normal American guy?

    E Facebook's future

    F Private! Be careful!

G Real friendship in the virtual world?
H Facebook's early days

lines 1–8	lines 9–20	lines 21–29	lines 30–36	lines 37–46	lines 47–55	lines 56–64
D	H	A	~~E~~ C	B	F	G

2. **Write down the sentence from the text which tells you that …** 4

   a) you can watch a film about Mark Zuckerberg at the cinema.

   A movie has been made about him L.6

   b) Facebook has many users.

   Today, around 700 million people have Facebook accounts L: 21-22

   c) it is not difficult to contact people through Facebook.

   _____

   d) some people are careless with their data.

   _____

3. **Answer the questions using information from the text. Write short answers.** 6

   a) Where did Mark Zuckerberg spend his childhood?

   _____

   b) What was the name of the network which he made for his family?

   _____

   c) When did Mark Zuckerberg start Facebook?

   _____

   d) How does Facebook get the money to pay its employees?

   _____

   e) You can communicate with your friends without going online. Write down two examples from the text.

   _____

   _____

D Text Production (Dictionaries are allowed.)

Choose either I. (Correspondence) or II. (Picture-based Writing). 16

I. Correspondence: E-Mail

Beachte: Deine E-Mail sollte 10 bis 12 Sätze umfassen bzw. 80 bis 100 Wörter beinhalten. Du kannst auch eigene Gedanken einbringen.
Denke an Anrede und Grußformel.

Angaben zur E-Mail: In einem Campingurlaub hast du Luca aus Italien kennen gelernt. Ihr wolltet in Kontakt bleiben. Nachdem er abgereist ist, entdeckst du, dass er sein Handy vergessen hat. Daraufhin schreibst du ihm eine E-Mail auf Englisch.

- Frage, wie es ihm geht.
- Teile mit, dass du sein Handy gefunden hast: wann, wo, ...
- Schlage vor, wie er sein Handy zurückbekommen kann.
- Frage, ob er damit einverstanden ist oder ob er eine andere Idee hat.
- Bedaure, dass er vor dir abgereist ist.
- Erkundige dich nach seiner Rückreise.
- Erzähle, was du nach seiner Abreise noch unternommen hast, z. B. Sport, Ausflüge, ...
- Sage, dass du im Anhang Fotos mitschickst.
- Füge hinzu, dass du gerne Fotos von ihm bekommen möchtest.
- Bitte ihn, dir bald zu antworten.

II. Picture-based Writing: Picture story

Betrachte die Bilder und schreibe eine Geschichte auf Englisch.
Beachte: Dein Text sollte 10 bis 12 Sätze umfassen bzw. 80 bis 100 Wörter beinhalten.
Du kannst auch eigene Gedanken einbringen.

The Wallet
Last month Anna and Julia went to a department store. Anna wanted to look for a dress for the school-leaving party. She saw a nice one and wanted to try it on. The girls went to the changing rooms.

Lösungen

A Listening Comprehension Test

(Die folgenden Dialoge hörst du je zweimal. Achte genau auf die Anweisungen. Versuche, die Aufgaben selbstständig zu lösen und sieh die Lösungen erst nach Bearbeitung der Aufgaben an.)

Part 1: Jenny is in a taxi on her way to the airport. While listening fill in the missing numbers. (Höchstpunktzahl: 4 Punkte)

1. 11.30
2. 5
3. £ 23.50
4. 10.45

Part 2: Jenny is checking in at the British Airways desk. While listening tick (✓) the correct ending. (Höchstpunktzahl: 3 Punkte)

1. a) ✓ ... a bag and a suitcase
2. a) ✓ ... 17 kilos.
3. b) ✓ ... a middle seat.

Part 3: At the gate Jenny hears an announcement. There's one mistake in each sentence. While listening cross out the wrong word. (Höchstpunktzahl: 4 Punkte)

1. ~~booked~~: checked in
2. ~~small~~: short
3. ~~pilots~~: engineers
4. ~~sit~~: stay

Part 4: At the gate a young woman talks to Jenny. Are the sentences true (T) or false (F)? While listening tick (✓) the correct box. (Höchstpunktzahl: 4 Punkte)

		T	F
1.	Jenny has been on holiday in England.		✓
2.	In Brighton Jenny stayed with friends		✓
3.	Jenny has been in England for two weeks now.	✓	
4.	In London Jenny visited a music school		✓

5. In the evening Jenny set her alarm clock. ☐ ✓
6. Jenny didn't have any breakfast. ✓ ☐
7. Jenny's taxi driver was very nice. ✓ ☐
8. Jenny hasn't got time to go to the airport café. ✓ ☐

B Use of English

(Diesen Prüfungsteil musst du ohne das Wörterbuch bearbeiten. Anhand der folgenden Aufgaben werden dein Wortschatz, deine Ausdrucksfähigkeit in kommunikativen Situationen sowie deine Grammatik-Kenntnisse beurteilt.)

1. **Computers**
   Complete the text. Use four different words from the box. There is an example at the beginning (0). (Höchstpunktzahl 4 Punkte)

   Every day I <u>turn on</u> my computer. Sometimes I <u>need</u> it for my homework because we often have to <u>write</u> texts. Once I lost an important text so now I always <u>save</u> everything immediately. There are also a lot of photos on my computer. I <u>send</u> the nicest ones to my friends.

2. **At a restaurant**
   Write the word that matches the definition. There is an example at the beginning (0). (Höchstpunktzahl 4 Punkte)

   a). menu
   b) bill
   c) kitchen
   d) knife

3. **Sounds**
   Find the word from the box which sounds the same. Write it on the line. There is an example at the beginning (0). (Höchstpunktzahl: 4 Punkte)
   (Zu Hause kannst du dir die einzelnen Wörter laut vorsprechen, dann fallen dir Gemeinsamkeiten in der Aussprache leichter auf.)

   a) there – pair
   b) own – stone
   c) said – bread
   d) why – pie

4. **In London**
   Fill in the words in their right form. There is an example at the beginning (0). (Höchstpunktzahl: 4 Punkte)
   (Hier sollst du die richtige Steigerungsform des jeweiligen Adjektivs einsetzen.)

   London is the <u>biggest</u> city in England. The London Underground is the <u>oldest</u> underground system in the world. People use it because it is <u>faster</u> than the buses. Taking a taxi is <u>more expensive</u> than using public transport. One of the <u>best</u> ways to get around the centre of London is on foot.

5. **A day out**
   Tell the story in the <u>simple past</u>. Use six different words from the box. There is an example at the beginning (0). (Höchstpunktzahl: 6 Punkte)
   (Wähle jeweils das passende Verb aus und setze es in die *simple past*-Form.)

   Yesterday Susan <u>met</u> her friend Beth in town. First the girls <u>went</u> to a café and <u>had</u> a milkshake. Then they <u>did</u> some shopping. They <u>spent</u> an hour in a clothes shop but they <u>didn't buy</u> anything. Later they <u>watched</u> an interesting film at the cinema.

6. **Different situations**
   What would you say? Tick (✓) the correct box. There is an example at the beginning (0). (Höchstpunktzahl: 3 Punkte)
   (Hier musst du jeweils die richtige Antwort oder Reaktion auf eine Frage oder Aussage ankreuzen.)

   a) ✓ Good idea.
   b) ✓ You're welcome. *(Bitte./Gern geschehen.)*
   c) ✓ Fine, thanks.

C   Reading Comprehension Test
(In diesem Prüfungsteil darfst du ein zweisprachiges Wörterbuch benutzen.)

1. **Find the correct title (A–H) for each part of the text. Use each letter only once. One title is already matched. There is one extra title.**
   (Höchstpunktzahl 6 Punkte)

lines 1–8	lines 9–20	lines 21–29	lines 30–36	lines 37–46	lines 47–55	lines 56–64
D	H	A	C	B	F	G

2. **Write down the sentence from the text which tells you that ...**

(Höchstpunktzahl 4 Punkte)

(Markiere im Text die Sätze, die das Gleiche bedeuten wie die angegebenen Sätze, und schreibe sie auf.)

a) A movie has been made about him.
(Z. 6)

b) (Today) around 700 million people have Facebook accounts.
oder: (He started) a company that millions of people all over the world use.
(Z. 21 f. und Z. 4 ff.)

c) You can contact individuals and groups easily.
(Z. 31 f.)

d) Of course there are some users who aren't worried about protecting their data.
oder: They don't mind if everyone can see them and read about them.
(Z. 49 ff.)

3. **Answer the questions using information from the text.**
   Write short answers. (Höchstpunktzahl 6 Punkte)

(Lies den Text noch einmal durch und beantworte die Fragen in Stichpunkten oder kurzen Sätzen.)

a) (near) New York (City)
(Z. 12 f.)

b) ZuckNet
(Z. 15)

c) in 2003
(Z. 17)

d) Facebook passes on data to other companies.
(Z. 44)
oder:
(through) advertisements /advertising
(Z. 39 ff.)

e) telephone
face-to-face conversation
handwritten letter(s)
(Z. 60 ff. Im Text sind drei Möglichkeiten erwähnt, von denen du zwei angeben musst.)

D Text Production

(Auch in diesem Prüfungsteil darfst du ein zweisprachiges Wörterbuch verwenden. Entscheide dich bei der Bearbeitung <u>entweder</u> für die E-mail <u>oder</u> für die Bildergeschichte.)

1. Correspondence: E-Mail   (Höchstpunktzahl: 16 Punkte)

(In der Aufgabenstellung findest du Vorgaben zum Inhalt der E-mail. Baue alle Vorgaben in deinen Text ein. Hier und da sollst du eigene Ideen hinzufügen, z. B. über den Fundort des Handys. Da du einem Freund / einer Urlaubsbekanntschaft schreibst, kannst du Umgangssprache verwenden.)

Hi Luca,

How are you? I hope you are fine. My family and I returned from Italy yesterday. Guess what I found on the day you left: your mobile phone! When I went to the beach I saw it on the bench that we had sat on. I could send you the mobile by post. Is that OK with you or do you have another idea?

I'm sorry that you had to go home one week before I did. It was pretty boring after that. How was your trip home? I hope you had a good journey.

After you left I spent most of the time with my family. We visited some of the nearby towns and went shopping. I also went jogging every day.

I attached the photos I took on your last day. I think they are quite funny. Please also send me the photos that you have taken.

I hope to hear from you soon!

Bye,

Emily

2. Picture-based Writing: Picture story   (Höchstpunktzahl: 16 Punkte)

(Bevor du mit dem Schreiben beginnst, solltest du die Abbildungen genau betrachten. Verwende die inhaltlichen Vorgaben, die du in den Sprechblasen findest, in deinem Text und arbeite den Hauptteil sowie das Ende der Geschichte aus.)

Vokabelhinweis:
1 to lend: (ver)leihen

… Anna was trying on the dress when Julia suddenly saw a wallet. It was under the bench of the changing room. Julia looked inside the wallet and found a card with the name "David Brown" on it and a mobile phone number. At the same time Anna saw the price tag of the dress. It cost 99 pounds! Anna didn't have so much money. So she had to put back the dress. Anna looked at other dresses that cost less. But she didn't like any of them. In the meantime, Julia called Mr Brown. She said: "Hello, is that Mr Brown? I found your wallet!" He was very happy and answered: "Let's meet at the café at 3 pm." When Anna and Julia met Mr Brown to give him his wallet, he gave each girl 20 pounds. The girls were very excited. Julia lent[1] Anna her 20 pounds. With the extra money Anna could buy the nice dress after all.

Notenschlüssel

Notenstufen	1	2	3	4	5	6
Punkte	72–64	63,5–52	51,5–39	38,5–25	24,5–12	11,5–0

Listening Comprehension Text

Part 1:
RECEPTIONIST: Hi, can I help you?
PAUL: Hi, yeah, we wanted to know if we can book a boat trip.
ALISON: And maybe you could recommend one to us.
RECEPTIONIST: Sure. A lot of our guests do this one. *(Gets a brochure and opens it.)*
ALISON: Oh, dolphins!
RECEPTIONIST: Yeah. This is a four-hour trip to watch the wild dolphins and their babies.
PAUL: Great, and can we go in the water, too?
RECEPTIONIST: Yeah, you can go snorkeling but not where the dolphins are, of course.
PAUL: Yeah, OK. And are there trips every day?
RECEPTIONIST: Yeah, every day, leaving at nine o'clock and getting back at around 1.30.
ALISON: OK. And how much does it cost?
RECEPTIONIST: Well, it's usually $95 over the phone and 90 over the internet, but we can do it for you for 85.
PAUL: OK.
ALISON: And do we have to book in advance?
RECEPTIONIST: You do, I'm afraid. The day before. Tomorrow's trip is almost full but there's still space on Friday.
PAUL: OK, we'll think about it and let you know.

Part 2:
TV MAN: OK, and let's have a look at the weather coming up over the next three days. Today it's going to be partly cloudy with temperatures steady at around 75 Fahrenheit. The chance of rain is about 20 % and the easterly winds are going to be between 15 to 20 mph.
Tomorrow, Thursday, it's going to feel quite breezy, too, with easterly winds between 25 to 30 mph. There's going to be a mix of sunshine and clouds. The chance of rain will be around 30 %, but all in all it'll feel warm out there with temperatures reaching a high of 85.
Moving on to Friday now. Friday's going to start clear and bright but with easterly winds reaching 35 mph there's a 50 % chance of rain by the late afternoon. Temperatures are going to climb to a maximum of 95 and it's going to feel pretty humid, too.

OK, so after the break, we'll be welcoming a special guest because *(fade begins here)* City Manager Billy Wardlow will be here to talk about the new parking regulations that are being introduced next year and what they're going to mean.

Part 3:
RECEPTIONIST: Hello there.
PAUL/ALISON: Hi.
RECEPTIONIST: Made up your mind about the boat trip yet?
PAUL: Yeah, we'd like to book for tomorrow if that's possible.
RECEPTIONIST: Oh, I'm sorry but tomorrow's trip's been cancelled. Because of the bad weather. How about Saturday?
ALISON: We're leaving on Saturday. Tomorrow's our last day.
RECEPTIONIST: Have you thought about going to *SeaWorld?*
PAUL: But that's quite a long way, isn't it?
RECEPTIONIST: Yeah, you're right, about 140 miles, so about 2 hours by car.
ALISON: Do you really want to be sitting in a car for four hours if we've got a 10-hour flight the next day.
PAUL: No, you're right.
ALISON: I'd rather be here tomorrow.
PAUL: And today? What else could we do?
RECEPTIONIST: Have you ever tried parasailing – you know, in a parachute from behind a boat?
ALISON: That sounds cool!
RECEPTIONIST: You can do it together – tandem parasailing.
PAUL: Locally?
RECEPTIONIST: Yes, there's a place about ten minutes on foot from here. I'll show you on the map where it is.
ALISON: Great. Then we can walk down there and check it out.
PAUL: That's a good idea.

Part 4:
SUNRISE: Hi, how can I help?
ALISON: Hi, I wanted to ask if we can join one of your trips today.

SUNRISE: Sure. When do you want to go?
ALISON: Well, this afternoon would be great.
SUNRISE: How about 2 o'clock. Or 3 o'clock?
ALISON: Two's fine. Do we need to bring anything special with us?
SUNRISE: Well the usual stuff – a towel, sunscreen and sunglasses. Oh, and your camera, of course.
ALISON: And do you need to see our passports?
SUNRISE: No, no.
ALISON: No identification or anything?
SUNRISE: No, just the name of the hotel where you're staying.

ALISON: OK. Um ... oh yes: my boyfriend's a bit scared of heights so I wanted to know how high up we go.
SUNRISE: About 500 feet – but that's the maximum.
ALISON: Okay. And how long is the trip?
SUNRISE: About 45 minutes, and you're up in the air for about 10 minutes. But your boyfriend needn't worry. You'll be up there with him holding his hand!
Alison: True. I'll tell him that.

A Listening Comprehension Test   points

Task 1: Alison and Paul are on holiday in Florida, USA. One morning they talk to the receptionist in their hotel.
While listening, tick (✓) the correct box. There is an example at the beginning (0).   5

0. Alison wants the receptionist to ... a boat trip.
   - [ ] book
   - [ ] choose
   - [✓] recommend
   - [ ] pay for

1. On the boat trip, Alison and Paul can ...
   - [ ] feed dolphins.
   - [ ] play with dolphins.
   - [ ] touch dolphins.
   - [✓] watch dolphins.

2. On the trip, Alison and Paul can also go ...
   - [ ] diving.
   - [ ] fishing.
   - [✓] snorkeling.
   - [ ] surfing.

3. The trip is from ...
   - [ ] 8 to 11.30.
   - [ ] 8 to 1.30.
   - [ ] 9 to 11.30.
   - [✓] 9 to 1.30.

4. Alison and Paul will have to pay …
   - [ ] $80.
   - [x] $85.
   - [ ] $90.
   - [ ] $95.
5. The receptionist says Alison and Paul could go on the trip …
   - [ ] today.
   - [ ] tomorrow.
   - [x] on Friday.
   - [ ] on Saturday.

Task 2: In the evening Alison and Paul listen to the weather forecast. Listen and complete the table.

	Temperature in Fahrenheit (°F)	Chance of rain in percent (%)	Winds in miles per hour (mph)
Today	75	20%	15–20
Thursday	85	30%	25–30
Friday	95	50	35

Part 3: The next day Alison and Paul talk to the receptionist again. Are the sentences true (T) or false (F)? While listening, tick (✓) the correct box. There is an example at the beginning (0).

		T	F
0.	Alison and Paul have made plans for today.		✓
1.	Today's boat trip has been cancelled.		✓
2.	Alison and Paul are leaving on Saturday.	✓	
3.	It's 240 miles to *SeaWorld*.		✓
4.	Alison and Paul want to try a sport together.	✓	
5.	The place is only ten minutes away by car.		✓

Part 4: Alison talks to a woman from *Sunrise Watersports*.
What do Alison and Paul have to bring with them (✓)? What do they **not** have to bring with them (✗)? Put a (✓) or a (✗) <u>in each box</u>. There is an example at the beginning (0).

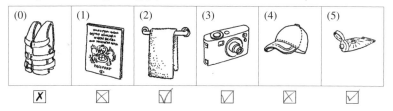

(0)	(1)	(2)	(3)	(4)	(5)
✗	✗	✓	✓	✗	✓

B Use of English

1. A British student talks about his last holidays.

> cloths – ~~clothes~~ – counties – countries – languages –
> ~~months~~ – nationalities – people – scenes – ~~sights~~

Read the text and fill in the word from the box that fits.
There is an example at the beginning (0).

Last year I travelled around the world for three (**0**) **months** in *June, July and August*.

I went to *Japan, India, the USA* and a lot of other (**1**) countries. Of all the cities I saw I liked New York best. When I was there I visited *the Empire State Building, the Statue of Liberty, Times Square* and many other well-known (**2**) sights. I went to a fashion store and bought a *jacket, trousers, a shirt* and other (**3**) clothes which are cheaper than in England. New York was full of tourists. I heard them speak *French, Chinese, Russian* and many other (**4**) languages.

2. Two tourists talk about their plans for the evening.
Write a word with the <u>same meaning</u> as the one in brackets.
There is an example at the beginning (0).

Woman: When does the show (**0** end) **finish** this evening?
Man: At about 10 o'clock.
Woman: (**1** Perhaps) Maybe we can have dinner somewhere afterwards.

Man:	Good idea.	
Woman:	Are there any restaurants close to the theatre?	
Man:	I don't think so. But we can (**2** go on foot) __walk__ somewhere.	
Woman:	No, let's (**3** get) __take__ a taxi.	
Man:	OK.	
Woman:	And let's (**4** reserve) __book__ a table.	

3. **Jack talks about his favourite hobby.** 4
   Write the correct form of the given word. There is an example at the beginning (0).

   At the age of ten I (**0** learn) **learned** how to surf. When I got my own board I (**1** be) __was__ so happy. Now I'm not only good at (**2** surf) __surfing__. I'm also a very good swimmer. Every weekend my friend Mike and I meet at a lake. Often we race against each other and Mike usually (**3** win) __wins__. At the moment I'm saving for a special course in Spain. I hope that I (**4** have) __will have__ enough money next year.

4. **Jack and Tina go to London for a weekend.** 4
   Complete the sentences using the correct word from the box. You do not need all the words. There is an example at the beginning (0).

   > at – ~~because~~ – ~~has~~ – had – ~~in~~ – on – our – ~~their~~ – ~~to~~ – while – why

   Jack and his sister Tina spent a weekend (**0**) **in** London. When they got (**1**) __to__ the station, Jack carried his sister's suitcase (**2**) __because__ it was so heavy. They took the Underground to (**3**) __their__ aunt. She lives in a small flat all by herself and she is a great cook. Whenever she (**4**) __has__ guests, she likes to cook for them.

5. **Tina wants to visit the Tower of London. She asks a Londoner for help** 4
   Complete the dialogue. There is an example at the beginning (0).

Tina:	Excuse me? (**0**) **Can you help me**?
Londoner:	Yes, of course.
Tina:	(**1**) __Is there a bus__ to the Tower?
Londoner:	Yes, it's bus number 15.
Tina:	How long (**2**) __does it take__ to get there?

Londoner: Not long. About twenty minutes.
Tina: How (3) much is it ?
Londoner: I'm not sure but the driver will know the price.
Tina: (4) Do you know if there's a bus stop nearby?
Londoner: Yes, just around the corner.
Tina: Thank you.
Londoner: No worries.

Reading Comprehension Test: Bethany Hamilton

1 Have you ever heard of Bethany Hamilton? Born on the island of Kauai, Hawaii, Bethany began surfing when she was five years old. **(0)** _____ Kauai is an ideal location for surfing and Bethany's older brothers, Noah and Timmy, are great surfers, too. Bethany's parents soon realized that their
5 youngest child had a special talent. In 1998, when she was eight, Bethany took part in her first state-wide surf competition and won. From then on, Bethany's passion for riding waves never left her.

On October 31, 2003, Bethany's life changed dramatically. While surfing near Kauai's North Shore she was attacked by a 15-foot tiger shark and lost
10 her left arm. It looked as if the career of a rising US surf star was suddenly over.

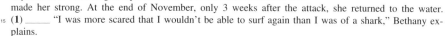

But it wasn't over. Bethany recovered quickly – both physically and mentally. Her love of surfing, her positive attitude to life and her faith in God made her strong. At the end of November, only 3 weeks after the attack, she returned to the water.
15 **(1)** _____ "I was more scared that I wouldn't be able to surf again than I was of a shark," Bethany explains.

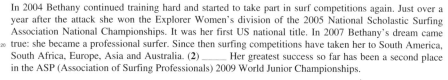

In 2004 Bethany continued training hard and started to take part in surf competitions again. Just over a year after the attack she won the Explorer Women's division of the 2005 National Scholastic Surfing Association National Championships. It was her first US national title. In 2007 Bethany's dream came
20 true: she became a professional surfer. Since then surfing competitions have taken her to South America, South Africa, Europe, Asia and Australia. **(2)** _____ Her greatest success so far has been a second place in the ASP (Association of Surfing Professionals) 2009 World Junior Championships.

Bethany is not only a star in the water. **(3)** _____ She has written an autobiography – a *New York Times* bestseller. There has been a documentary about her on TV and last year a Hollywood movie was made
25 about her: in *Soul Surfer* Bethany is played by the US actress Anna Sophia Robb. Bethany often gives interviews to journalists and television networks. She tells her inspiring story at schools, colleges and churches. With her family, she started a foundation. *Friends of Bethany* (www.friendsofbethany.com) is a non-profit organization that supports shark attack survivors and other amputees worldwide.

Bethany has come a long way since 2003 – from a teenage girl who wanted to be a professional surfer to
30 a 21-year-old professional surfer who is an idol of inspiration and hope. **(4)** _____ This is what she has to say to young people: "Do your best in life, find the good in bad situations, be kind to others and try not to be too cool!"

To keep up on Bethany's adventures you can read her blog and follow her travels at bethanyhamilton.com.

© Text copyright 2011, based on: www.bethanyhamilton.com, reprinted and adapted by permission

Qualifizierender Hauptschulabschluss – Englisch 2012

C Reading Comprehension Test (Dictionary allowed.)

1. **Find the correct title (A–G) for each paragraph in the text. There is one extra title. One title is already matched.** 5

   A A face in the media
   B A hero for young people
   C A terrible accident
   D Back on the surfboard
   E Bethany's childhood
   F The end of a career
   G Turning professional

paragraph 1 (lines 1–7)	paragraph 2 (lines 8–11)	paragraph 3 (lines 12–16)	paragraph 4 (lines 17–22)	paragraph 5 (lines 23–28)	paragraph 6 (lines 29–33)
E	C	D	G	A	B

2. **Four sentences are missing in the text.** 4
   Read the sentences (A–F) and match them with the gaps in the text (1–4). There is one extra sentence. There is an example at the beginning (0).

   A All over the world Bethany has competed with the best.
   B That's not so surprising.
   C Out of the water she has been successful, too.
   D Through her sport, Bethany has reached millions of people with her message.
   E Bethany was absolutely hopeless.
   F Was she scared?

(0)	(1)	(2)	(3)	(4)
B	F	A	C	D

3. **Are the sentences true (T) or false (F)?** 4
   There is an example at the beginning (0).

	T	F
Example: Bethany was a teenager when she started surfing.		✓
a) Bethany's brothers can surf well.	✓	
b) The shark attack took Bethany's right arm.		✓
c) Bethany returned to the water a long time after the attack.		✓
d) Bethany tells people to think positively about life.	✓	

E 2012-7

4. **Which line(s) from the text tell(s) you that …**
   There is an example at the beginning.

   Example: Kauai is a very good place for surfing. **line 3**

   a) Bethany's mom and dad saw that she was very good at surfing.

   b) Bethany's life was different from one moment to the next.

   c) Bethany is a religious person.

   d) Bethany has told her life story in a book.

a)	b)	c)	d)
line(s) 5	line(s) 8	line(s) 13	line(s) 23

5. **Answer the questions using information from the text. Write short answers. There is an example at the beginning.**

   Example: Where was Bethany born? **on Kauai**

   a) When did Bethany first become a US national champion?
      _2005_

   b) What's the title of the film about Bethany's life?
      Soul Surfer

   c) Which group of people does Bethany's foundation help?
      Give one example.
      shark attack survivors

D Text Production (Dictionary allowed.)

Choose either I. (Correspondence) or II. (Picture story). **20**

I. Correspondence: E-Mail

Beachte: Deine E-Mail sollte ungefähr **12** Sätze umfassen bzw. etwa **100** Wörter beinhalten. Du kannst auch eigene Gedanken einbringen.

Denke an Anrede, Schlusssatz, Grußformel und an eine ansprechende äußere Form.

Schreibe an deine/n Freund/in Chris eine E-Mail auf Englisch. Gehe dabei auf folgende Inhalte ein:

- Berichte von deiner Teilnahme an einem internationalen Fußballcamp letzten Sommer.
- Sage, in welcher Stadt es stattgefunden hat und wie lange du dort warst.
- Gehe auf **drei** Programmpunkte ein, z. B.
  - die Besichtigung des Stadions
  - die Möglichkeit, berühmte Fußballstars persönlich zu treffen
  - das Training mit professionellen Fußballtrainern
  - Ausflüge, Diskobesuch, Einkaufen …
- Beschreibe, was dir besonders gefallen hat, z. B. die Gelegenheit, Jungen und Mädchen aus aller Welt kennenzulernen.
- Schreibe, dass du vorhast, dich wieder für dieses Camp zu bewerben.
- Frage, ob er/sie auch mitkommen möchte.
- Mache ihn/sie auf die Informationen im Internet aufmerksam.

II. Creative Writing: Picture story

Betrachte die Bilder und schreibe eine Geschichte auf Englisch.
Beachte: Deine Geschichte sollte ungefähr **12** Sätze umfassen bzw. etwa **100** Wörter beinhalten. Achte auf eine ansprechende äußere Form.
Du kannst wie folgt beginnen:

Shark alarm
Paul always wanted to have a remote-controlled shark. Last year …

Lösungen

A Listening Comprehension Test

Task 1: Alison and Paul are on holiday in Florida, USA. One morning they talk to the receptionist in their hotel.
While listening, tick (✓) the correct box. (Höchstpunktzahl: 5 Punkte)

1. ✓ watch dolphins.
2. ✓ snorkeling.
3. ✓ 9 to 1.30.
4. ✓ $ 85.
5. ✓ on Friday.

Task 2: In the evening Alison and Paul listen to the weather forecast.
Listen and complete the table. (Höchstpunktzahl: 5 Punkte)

	Temperature in Fahrenheit (°F)	Chance of rain in percent (%)	Winds in miles per hour (mph)
Today	75	20	15–20
Thursday	85	30	25–30
Friday	95	50	35

Task 3: The next day Alison and Paul talk to the receptionist again. Are the sentences true (T) or false (F)? While listening, tick (✓) the correct box.
(Höchstpunktzahl: 5 Punkte)

	T	F
1. Today's boat trip has been cancelled.		✓
2. Alison and Paul are leaving on Saturday.	✓	
3. It's 240 miles to *SeaWorld*.		✓
4. Alison and Paul want to try a sport together.	✓	
5. The place is only ten minutes away by car.		✓

E 2012-11

Task 4: Alison talks to a woman from *Sunrise Watersports*. What do Alison and Paul have to bring with them (✓)? What do they not have to bring with them (✗)? Put a (✓) or a (✗) in each box. (Höchstpunktzahl: 5 Punkte)

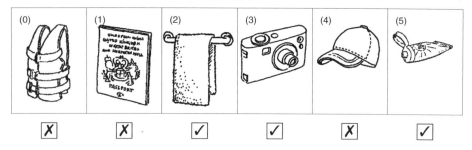

(0)	(1)	(2)	(3)	(4)	(5)
✗	✗	✓	✓	✗	✓

B Use of English

(In diesem Teil werden dein Wortschatz und deine Grammatik-Kenntnisse geprüft. Sind bei einer Aufgabe Wörter bereits vorgegeben, achte beim Einsetzen des ausgewählten Wortes in die Lücke darauf, das Wort richtig zu schreiben. Abschreibfehler führen nämlich zu Punktverlust, den du mit etwas Sorgfalt vermeiden kannst.)

1. **A British student talks about his last holidays. Read the text and fill in the word from the box that fits.** (Höchstpunktzahl: 4 Punkte)

Last year I travelled around the world for three <u>months</u> in *June, July and August*. I went to *Japan, India, the USA* and a lot of other <u>countries</u>. Of all the cities I saw I like New York best. When I was there I visited *the Empire State Building, the Statue of Liberty, Times Square* and many other well-known <u>sights</u>. I went to a fashion store and bought a *jacket, trousers, a shirt* and other <u>clothes</u> which are cheaper than in England. New York was full of tourists. I heard them speak *French, Chinese, Russian* and many other <u>languages</u>.

2. **Two tourists talk about their plans for the evening. Write a word with the <u>same meaning</u> as the one in brackets.**
(Höchstpunktzahl: 4 Punkte)

WOMAN: When does the show <u>finish</u> this evening?
MAN: At about 10 o'clock.
WOMAN Maybe we can have dinner somewhere afterwards.
MAN: Good idea.
WOMAN: Are there any restaurants close to the theatre?
MAN: I don't think so. But we can <u>walk</u> somewhere.
WOMAN: No, let's <u>take</u> / call a taxi.

E 2012-12

| MAN: | OK. |
| WOMAN: | And let's <u>book</u> a table. |

3. **Jack talks about his favourite hobby. Write the correct form of the given word.** (Höchstpunktzahl: 4 Punkte)

At the age of ten I <u>learned</u> how to surf. When I got my own board I <u>was</u> so happy. Now I'm not only good at <u>surfing</u>. I'm also a very good swimmer. Every weekend my friend Mike and I meet at a lake. Often we race against each other and Mike usually <u>wins</u>. At the moment I'm saving for a special course in Spain. I hope that I <u>'ll have</u> / <u>will have</u> enough money next year.

4. **Jack and Tina go to London for a weekend. Complete the sentences using the correct word from the box. You do not need all the words.** (Höchstpunktzahl: 4 Punkte)

Jack and his sister Tina spent a weekend <u>in</u> London. When they got <u>to</u> the station, Jack carried his sister's suitcase <u>because</u> it was so heavy. They took the Underground to <u>their</u> aunt. She lives in a small flat all by herself and she is a great cook. Whenever she <u>has</u> guests, she likes to cook for them.

5. **Tina wants to visit the Tower of London. She asks a Londoner for help. Complete the dialogue.** (Höchstpunktzahl: 4 Punkte)

TINA:	Excuse me? <u>Can you help me</u>?
LONDONER:	Yes, of course.
TINA:	<u>Is there a bus</u> / <u>Is this the bus</u> / <u>Could you tell me if there is a bus</u> / <u>Do you know if there is a bus</u> to the Tower?
LONDONER:	Yes, it's bus number 15.
TINA:	How long <u>does it take</u> / <u>will it take</u> / <u>will it be</u> to get there?
LONDONER:	Not long. About twenty minutes.
TINA:	How <u>much is it</u> / <u>much does it cost</u> / <u>much is the ticket</u>?
LONDONER:	I'm not sure but the driver will know the price.
TINA:	<u>Do you know</u> / <u>Would you tell me</u> / <u>Could you tell me</u> if there's a bus stop nearby?
LONDONER:	Yes, just around the corner.
TINA:	Thank you.
LONDONER:	No worries.

C Reading Comprehension Test

(In diesem Teil darfst du ein Wörterbuch verwenden)

Vokabelhinweise: Z. 6: to take part in: teilnehmen an; Z. 6: state-wide surf competition: Surf-Wettbewerb mit Teilnehmern aus den einzelnen Bundesstaaten der USA; Z. 7: passion: Leidenschaft; Z. 9: 15-foot tiger shark: 4,5 m langer Tigerhai; Z. 12: to recover: sich erholen; Z. 12: physically: körperlich; Z. 12 f.: mentally: seelisch; Z. 13: attitude: Einstellung; Z. 13: faith: Glaube; Z. 21: success: Erfolg; Z. 27: foundation: Stiftung; Z. 28: non-profit: gemeinnützig, nicht auf Gewinn ausgerichtet; Z. 28: to support: unterstützen; Z. 28: survivor: Überlebende(r)

1. Find the correct title (A–G) for each paragraph in the text.

   (Höchstpunktzahl: 5 Punkte)

paragraph 1 (lines 1–7)	paragraph 2 (lines 8–11)	paragraph 3 (lines 12–16)	paragraph 4 (lines 17–22)	paragraph 5 (lines 23–28)	paragraph 6 (lines 29–33)
E	C	D	G	A	B

2. Four sentences are missing in the text. Read the sentences (A – F) and match them with the gaps in the text (1– 4).
   There is one extra sentence. (Höchstpunktzahl: 4 Punkte)

   Vokabelhinweise: to compete with: sich messen mit, gegen jmd. antreten; successful: erfolgreich; to be hopeless: ohne Hoffnung sein

(0)	(1)	(2)	(3)	(4)
B	F	A	C	D

3. Are the sentences true (T) or false (F)? (Höchstpunktzahl: 4 Punkte)

	T	F
a) Bethany's brothers can surf well.	✓	☐
b) The shark attack took Bethany's right arm.	☐	✓
c) Bethany returned to the water a long time after the attack.	☐	✓
d) Bethany tells people to think positively about life.	✓	☐

4. **Which line(s) from the text tell(s) you that ...** (Höchstpunktzahl: 4 Punkte)

a)	b)	c)	d)
lines 4–5	line 8	line 13	line 23

5. **Answer the questions using information from the text.**
   Write short answers. (Höchstpunktzahl: 3 Punkte)

   a) (in) 2005
      (Z. 18)

   b) (it's) Soul Surfer
      (Z. 25)

   c) shark attack survivors
      oder: (other) amputees (worldwide)
      (Z. 28)

D Text Production

(Auch in diesem Prüfungsteil darfst du ein zweisprachiges Wörterbuch verwenden. Entscheide dich bei der Bearbeitung entweder für die E-Mail oder für die Bildergeschichte.)

1. **Correspondence: E-Mail** (Höchstpunktzahl: 20 Punkte)

   (Berücksichtige beim Verfassen deiner E-Mail die allgemeinen Hinweise zu Umfang und Form, die in der Aufgabenstellung beschrieben sind. Verfasse eine verständliche E-Mail in ganzen Sätzen. Bringe beim Schreiben die Vorgaben zum Inhalt ein und ergänze sie, wenn du möchtest, auch durch eigene Gedanken.)

   Hi Chris,

   Would you like to take part in an international football (*oder AmE:* soccer) camp with me? I went to an international football camp in London last summer and it was great! I stayed there for two weeks and I was able to improve my skills a lot. It was the first time that I got training from professional trainers and I also met some football stars! Just imagine, I even shook hands with Theo Walcott and I also got some autographs!

   It was also great that I was able to meet other boys and girls from all over the world. At the weekends we went sightseeing in London. We visited the Emirates stadium, went shopping and one night we went to a fantastic disco.

   I am going to apply *(bewerben)* for the football camp again this year. Do you want to join me? You can find some more information on the internet: www.soccercampsinternational.com/arsenal-soccer-camp

I'm looking forward to hearing from you soon.

Best wishes,

Angela

2. Creative Writing: Picture story (Höchstpunktzahl: 20 Punkte)

(Sieh dir die Bilder genau an, bevor du mit dem Schreiben beginnst. Beachte auch die Aufschriften: „Happy birthday", „remote controlled shark" (ferngesteuerter Hai), „lifeguard" (Rettungsschwimmer), „Help!" und „Ron's pedal boat". Berücksichtige beim Schreiben der Bildergeschichte die allgemeinen Hinweise zu Umfang und Form, die in der Aufgabenstellung angegeben sind. Denke an Einleitung, Überleitung und Schluss und verwende in deinem Text auch die wörtliche Rede. Wie die Geschichte beginnen könnte, findest du ebenfalls auf dem Angabenblatt. Verfasse die Geschichte in der Zeitform simple past, Signalwort: last year)

Shark alarm

Paul always wanted to have a remote-controlled shark. Last year, on his birthday, he finally got one as a present from his parents. He was very happy. Paul took the shark with him the next time he went to the seaside. It was a sunny and warm day and some people were out on the sea in pedal boats. "The perfect moment to try my remote-controlled shark", Paul thought. He wanted to scare the people a little by letting the shark swim around their pedal boats. It worked wonderfully! Two ladies with hats got really frightened when they saw the shark's fin *(Flosse)* going around their boat. One of them threw her arms up into the air and the other one screamed "Help!" The life guard came right away and was very angry with Paul. "Leave the beach – now! You are not allowed to come back with your shark anymore!" he shouted. Paul was disappointed that the life guard didn't see the fun of it.

Notenschlüssel

Notenstufen	1	2	3	4	5	6
Punkte	80–68	67–55	54–41	40–27	26–13	12–0

Sicher durch alle Klassen!

Schülergerecht aufbereiteter Lernstoff mit anschaulichen Beispielen, abwechslungsreichen Übungen und erklärenden Lösungen. Schließt Wissenslücken, gibt Sicherheit und Motivation durch Erfolgserlebnisse.

Mathematik Hauptschule

Mathematik Grundwissen 5. Klasse	Best.-Nr. 934051
Mathematik Grundwissen 6. Klasse	Best.-Nr. 934061
Mathematik Grundwissen 7. Klasse	Best.-Nr. 93407
Mathematik Grundwissen 8. Klasse	Best.-Nr. 93408
Mathematik Grundwissen 9. Klasse	Best.-Nr. 93409
Übertritt Mathematik 4. Klasse	Best.-Nr. 9950401
Probearbeiten Mathematik 5. Klasse Hauptschule	Best.-Nr. 930001
Probearbeiten Mathematik 6. Klasse Hauptschule	Best.-Nr. 930002
Probearbeiten Mathematik 7. Klasse Hauptschule	Best.-Nr. 930003
Probearbeiten Mathematik 8. Klasse Hauptschule	Best.-Nr. 930004
Probearbeiten Mathematik 9. Klasse Hauptschule	Best.-Nr. 930005
Arbeitsheft Mathematik 5. Klasse Hauptschule Bayern	Best.-Nr. 9350051
Arbeitsheft Mathematik 6. Klasse Hauptschule Bayern	Best.-Nr. 9350061
Kompakt-Wissen Hauptschule Mathematik	Best.-Nr. 934001

Deutsch Hauptschule

Deutsch Grundwissen 5. Klasse	Best.-Nr. 93445
Deutsch Grundwissen 6. Klasse	Best.-Nr. 93446
Deutsch Grundwissen 7. Klasse	Best.-Nr. 93447
Deutsch Grundwissen 8. Klasse	Best.-Nr. 93448
Zeichensetzung 5.–7. Klasse	Best.-Nr. 934413
Deutsche Rechtschreibung 5.–10. Klasse	Best.-Nr. 934411
Diktat 5.–10. Klasse mit MP3-CD	Best.-Nr. 934412
Übertritt Deutsch 4. Klasse mit Audio-CD	Best.-Nr. 9954401
Arbeitsheft Deutsch als Zweitsprache Grundkurs Lernfeld 1: „Ich und du" mit MP3-CD	Best.-Nr. 1055401
Arbeitsheft Deutsch als Zweitsprache Grundkurs Lernfeld 2: „Lernen" mit MP3-CD	Best.-Nr. 1055403
Arbeitsheft Deutsch als Zweitsprache Grundkurs Lernfeld 3: „Sich orientieren" mit MP3-CD	Best.-Nr. 1055405
Kompakt-Wissen Hauptschule Deutsch Aufsatz	Best.-Nr. 934401

Jahrgangsstufentest 6. Klasse

Jahrgangsstufentest Mathematik 6. Klasse Hauptschule Bayern	Best.-Nr. 935061
Jahrgangsstufentest Deutsch 6. Klasse Hauptschule Bayern	Best.-Nr. 935461

Sprachenzertifikat

Sprachenzertifikat Englisch Niveau A 2 mit Audio-CD	Best.-Nr. 105552
Sprachenzertifikat Englisch Niveau B 1 mit Audio-CD	Best.-Nr. 105550

Englisch Hauptschule

Englisch Grundwissen 5. Klasse	Best.-Nr. 93455
Englisch Grundwissen 6. Klasse	Best.-Nr. 93456
Englisch Grundwissen 9. Klasse	Best.-Nr. 93451
Englisch Hörverstehen 9. Klasse mit MP3-CD	Best.-Nr. 93452
Klassenarbeiten Englisch 5. Klasse mit MP3-CD	Best.-Nr. 1035551
Klassenarbeiten Englisch 6. Klasse mit MP3-CD	Best.-Nr. 1035561
Arbeitsheft Bildungsstandards Englisch *Reading* Mittlerer Schulabschluss B 1	Best.-Nr. 101550
Kompakt-Wissen Hauptschule Englisch Themenwortschatz	Best.-Nr. 934501
Kompakt-Wissen Hauptschule Englisch Grundwortschatz	Best.-Nr. 934502

GSE · AWT

Geschichte · Sozialkunde · Erdkunde Grundwissen Quali Bayern	Best.-Nr. 93481
Arbeit · Wirtschaft · Technik Grundwissen Quali Bayern	Best.-Nr. 93485
Arbeitsheft Arbeit · Wirtschaft · Technik 9. Klasse Hauptschule Bayern	Best.-Nr. 9358501

VERA 8

VERA 8 – Mathematik Version A: Hauptschule	Best.-Nr. 935082
Arbeitsheft VERA 8 Mathematik Version A: Hauptschule	Best.-Nr. 9350001
VERA 8 – Deutsch Version A: Hauptschule mit MP3-CD	Best.-Nr. 935482
Arbeitsheft VERA 8 Deutsch Version A: Hauptschule mit MP3-CD	Best.-Nr. 9354005
VERA 8 – Englisch Version A: Hauptschule mit MP3-CD	Best.-Nr. 935582
Arbeitsheft VERA 8 Englisch Version A: Hauptschule mit MP3-CD	Best.-Nr. 9355005
ohne MP3-CD	Best.-Nr. 9355001

Ratgeber für Schüler

Richtig Lernen Tipps und Lernstrategien 5./6. Klasse	Best.-Nr. 10481
Richtig Lernen Tipps und Lernstrategien 7.–10. Klasse	Best.-Nr. 10482

(Bitte blättern Sie um)

Original-Prüfungsaufgaben und Training für die Prüfung

Training Quali 2013

- Ideal für die selbstständige Vorbereitung von Schülerinnen und Schülern der Klassen 8 und 9 auf den **Quali** an Hauptschulen in Bayern.
- Im **umfangreichen Trainingsteil** wird das Grundwissen intensiv wiederholt und dauerhaft gefestigt.
- Dazu Original-Prüfungsaufgaben zum Üben unter Prüfungsbedingungen.
- Mit ausführlichen, schülergerechten **Lösungsvorschlägen** zu allen Aufgaben im separaten Lösungsheft.
- Im übersichtlichen **Format A4**.

Training Quali Mathematik Bayern
■ .... Best.-Nr. 93503

Lösungsheft zu 93503
■ .... Best.-Nr. 93504

Training Quali Deutsch Bayern mit MP3-CD
■ .... Best.-Nr. 93545

Lösungsheft zu 93545
■ .... Best.-Nr. 93544

Training Quali Englisch Bayern mit MP3-CD
■ .... Best.-Nr. 93555

Lösungsheft zu 93555
■ .... Best.-Nr. 93554

Sammelband Training Quali Mathematik, Deutsch, Englisch Bayern
■ .... Best.-Nr. 93413

Lösungsheft zu 93413
■ .... Best.-Nr. 93414

Natürlich führen wir noch mehr Titel für alle Fächer und Stufen: Alle Informationen unter
www.stark-verlag.de

Abschluss-Prüfungsaufgaben

- Bewährte Unterstützung für Schülerinnen und Schüler bei der **selbstständigen Prüfungsvorbereitung**: Vom Kultusministerium in Bayern zentral gestellte Prüfungsaufgaben für den Quali und den Hauptschulabschluss 10. Klasse, einschließlich des aktuellen Jahrgangs.
- **Mit ausführlichen, schülergerechten Lösungen.**

Quali Mathematik Bayern
Format A5
■ .... Best.-Nr. 93500

Quali Deutsch Bayern
Format A5
■ .... Best.-Nr. 93540

Quali Englisch Bayern
Format A5
■ .... Best.-Nr. 93550

Sammelband Quali Mathematik, Deutsch, Englisch Bayern
Format A5
■ .... Best.-Nr. 93400

Abschlussprüfung Mathematik 10. Klasse M-Zug Bayern
Format A4
■ .... Best.-Nr. 93501

Abschlussprüfung Deutsch 10. Klasse M-Zug Bayern mit MP3-CD
Format A4
■ .... Best.-Nr. 93541

Abschlussprüfung Englisch 10. Klasse M-Zug Bayern mit MP3-CD
Format A4
■ .... Best.-Nr. 93551

Sammelband Abschlussprüfung Mathematik, Deutsch, Englisch 10. Klasse M-Zug Bayern
Format A4
■ .... Best.-Nr. 93410

Lernen ▪ Wissen ▪ Zukunft
STARK